It Went to the Dogs

How Michael Vick's Dogfighting Compound Became a Haven for Rescue Pups

WHO chains YOU
PUBLISHING

TAMIRA THAYNE

Published by Who Chains You Publishing
P.O. Box 581
Amissville, VA 20106

www.WhoChainsYou.com

Written and designed by Tamira Thayne
www.TamiraThayne.com

Expanded Edition Casebound ISBN: 978-1-946044-77-8

Printed in the United States of America

First Edition

To Dr. Leslie Dragon
Whose Courage in Speaking
Out Saved Lives

&

In Memory of
Ransom T. McCarty
and Peggy & Eric Lieber
For Their Generosity to the Chained Dogs

ALSO BY
Author Tamira Thayne

Foster Doggie Insanity

Capitol in Chains

The Chained Gods Series
The Wrath of Dog, The Curse of Cur,
The Knight's Chain, The King's Tether

The Animal Protector Series
Smidgey Pidgey's Predicament, Spittin' Kitten's
Speed-Away, Raffy Calfy's Rescue

Editor of The Rescue Smiles Series
Rescue Smiles, More Rescue Smiles

TABLE OF

Contents

Testimonials

"Because of Tamira's dedication, devotion, and strong convictions toward the plight of chained dogs, her dream of all dogs living free from chains has become a national and international movement. Her legacy continues through those who supported and were mentored by her, and were inspired to carry on her important work via their own anti-chaining organizations."
*—**Melody Whitworth**, former DDB Rep and founder, Unchained Melodies Dog Rescue*

"What a wonderful day I spent at the Good Newz Rehab Center in Smithfield, Virginia, founded by my friend Tamira Thayne. Her love for dogs and passionate fight for their rights moved me on a very deep level.

"Since I was there soon after the foundation took over, I was able to view and photograph the actual buildings Michael Vick used for his dog fighting ring.

"The photos portray a dark and frightening place marked by chains, blood, and a horrible cycle of life and death for so many pups. Being there in that space made me feel exactly the same way I did when I photographed Dachau concentration camp so many years before."*—**Rita Thomas**, photographer and Air Force veteran*

Axle from carpet mill in fighting shed. Photo by Rita Thomas.

Foreword

It was a feral cat and the internet that brought Tami and I together. I'm not even sure how our paths crossed, but I can remember her exact words: "Girl, you need to get that cat a litterbox." It was my first TNR and the vet appointment was still a week away. Little did I know that this would lead to a lifelong friendship that allowed me to be a part of a movement for the plight of chained and neglected dogs.

It was the very beginning of Dogs Deserve Better, and the word was spreading about the woman who was standing up for the dogs heard barking all night long in the cold, begging for help. The people who felt hopeless about the situation now had somewhere to turn. People from all over the country could connect with Tami and help educate themselves as well as the "chainers" about the abuse that was occurring.

It was a movement of kindness and compassion that I was

able to contribute to behind the scenes. It meant a lot, because I didn't have the balls to stand on the firing line like Tami—being a CPA and keeping the books in order was the perfect way to get involved.

Once I realized that I couldn't in fact release this sweet cat back outside to fend for himself, Tami stepped up to take the cat I'd named "Spirit". We lived three hours apart and met halfway, and our friendship and rescue coordination was born.

It is so true that everyone has a part to play, and all are vital in the success of an organization, even if you feel you aren't doing much. Tami was doing all of the heavy lifting, and I was merely reconciling the bank records, but it was something she couldn't do and it mattered.

At this point Dogs Deserve Better was being run out of Tami's house. She'd given up any and all luxuries to open her home as the headquarters and she was all in. From employees to foster dogs, her house was invaded with her new purpose in life.

She worked so hard to bring in every dollar to help pay for brochures to educate, or buy supplies to stuff doghouses with straw for even a little bit of warmth. She came up with a Valentine program idea wherein addresses were collected from people who lived near a chained dog, and she would pair these addresses with Valentines made by schoolchildren, a brochure about chaining, and a dog treat asking them to please release their dog.

She gave out HER phone number where she answered calls, even from angry and hateful recipients of those Valentines. But then there were the handful of calls where she'd gotten through to the person's heart, and that dog, for the first time in its life, was invited to live inside the family's home or relinquished to foster care because he or she deserved better.

She tolerated the hatred of thousands so she could rejoice in the few. The Valentine program grew to over 19,000 addresses per year, with representatives holding stuffing parties throughout the country. I should have known then that when Tami told me she had a crazy idea, there was no way she wasn't going to make it happen.

Over the next few years the organization grew, and eventually was too big to run out of her home; and let's face it, even the strongest person needs a little piece of space all to themselves. Tami hadn't had that since I'd met her.

Then the news hit about Michael Vick and his house of horrors at Bad Newz Kennels. I remember how devastated everyone was, and the camera footage on the news showing the poor dogs and the property they were tied to: all the barns painted black so that they couldn't be seen at night, all the trees camouflaging the dogs scattered about the acres and forced to live on heavy metal chains. It was an appalling story, brought to light only because of Michael Vick's celebrity.

Four years later, when she found out the property was still up for sale, Tami went to work. She told me flat out, "I'm going to move DDB to Bad Newz Kennels and change it to Good Newz. I say we rehabilitate formerly chained dogs in Vick's house and change the energy of that space. What do you think?"

Now, I had been to many of Tami's booths—where she would lug boxes of books, bumper stickers, and brochures, plus a big tent and tables, and spend 8-10 hours between set up and tear down—just to earn $100 bucks in donations. And those were the good events.

So when she told me Vick's house and grounds was listed at ONLY $595,000, and she would raise the money to buy the property, I should have known she would find a way. By then DDB had a decent amount of monthly subscribers, but my gosh, to raise $595,000? Ummm . . . right.

Then I watched her do it.

The rest is her story to tell.

—Deborah Carr, CPA,
former Dogs Deserve Better Treasurer

Introduction

"Human progress is neither automatic nor
inevitable . . . Every step toward the goal
of justice requires sacrifice, suffering, and
struggle; the tireless exertions and passionate concern of dedicated individuals."
—Martin Luther King, Jr.

The house sat empty, an eerie white sentinel against
the flat winter landscape, now guarding only whispers
of the past. A six-foot white metal fence with coded entry gate
lined the country road, abandoning its purpose at the property
line and allowing passage to all with the temerity and curiosity

to walk around.

The bullet hole in the front window went unnoticed.

I was alone, parked across the street, and early for my appointment with the Hampton Roads, Virginia, realtor. Today was the day I'd tour Michael Vick's former dogfighting compound, something I'd never imagined nor particularly wanted to do.

Seemed pretty creepy to me.

I felt the whispers surround me, reaching out. The rescuer in me wanted to rescue the ghosts, too; embrace the broken dogs who lay undiscovered and probably buried on the property, assure them they weren't forgotten. I shuddered, pulling myself together.

"That's stupid, Tami," I told myself. "There's nothing here but you and this house of torture; I'm sure there's no actual ghosts." Maybe I smirked, but was there anything really funny about it? Doubtful.

Maybe talking to yourself is just a recipe for amusement—or disaster, depending on your perspective.

It was the 1st of February, 2011, and I would be exploring Vick's former dogfighting compound for a surprising reason: the nonprofit organization I'd founded, Dogs Deserve Better, was considering buying the 15-acre property in Surry County, Virginia, and creating a haven for our rescued, formerly chained dogs there.

I fidgeted as I waited, equal parts trepidation and excitement. Would we, could we, should we buy a place not only with a history, but THIS KIND of HISTORY?

There was a lot to ponder. First on the agenda, however, was to ascertain if it was workable for our needs and worth the purchase price.

The back of the house.

Soon the realtor, along with Dogs Deserve Better supporter Monica S., a Virginia-based business owner—arrived and I would step onto the property where dogs had lived chained, were forced to fight, and then were brutally murdered for failing to impress Vick and his cohorts.

Was I up for the challenge?

And, more importantly, would I live to regret the decision I would ultimately make that chilly winter's day?

Maybe. It would all remain to be seen.

The view from the field where the dogs used to live chained, sheds in treeline.

CHAPTER ONE:

The Tour

"VICK TOOK THE NYLON CORD OFF OF THE HANGING DOG THAT WOULD NOT DIE. TOGETHER HE AND VICK LIFTED IT INTO THE AIR AND SLAMMED IT INTO THE GROUND, KILLING IT."
—CO-DEFENDANT QUANIS PHILLIPS [1]

What I remember about that first experience with the house and grounds of 1915 Moonlight Road was a stillness, a loneliness, an oppressive feel; yet underneath there was a yearning for more—a wish to be seen, to be heard. Did the land, the souls who remained on the property seek redemption for the blood spilled in their name? Perhaps.

Or, was I just projecting? . . . a real possibility, I would have to acknowledge. Yet I still can't shake the memory of wanting to protect the ground and all those lying therein, a similar desire to what one might experience when visiting battlefields or other sites of tragedy—a wish to somehow "fix" the horrors of the past.

That awareness would lead me to ultimately say "Yes" to uprooting my life and moving my organization from my Pennsylvania home to such unlikely, yet seemingly hallowed, grounds.

If you're unfamiliar with the full story behind the tragic occurrences on pro football player Michael Vick's Surry County, Virginia, property, I would urge you to read both *The Lost Dogs: Michael Vick's Dogs and their Tale of Rescue and Redemption* and *Badd Newz: The Untold Story of the Michael Vick Dog Fighting Case* before continuing my tale.

These two books lay out in stunning detail the scope of the treachery and underhanded dealings—going all the way to the top—in Surry County, Virginia that would enable Vick to set up a dogfighting operation and get away with it for as long as he did.

According to Jim Gorant, author of *The Lost Dogs*, Michael Vick was seven years old when he first saw dogs fighting in his Newport News neighborhood; by the time he was a teenager he was participating in the fights himself.[2]

As Vick left behind his background of poverty and entered the world of pro sports and the crazy money that comes with it, a thirst for dogfighting still coursed through his veins. When he started making bank as quarterback of the Atlanta Falcons, he purchased the 15-acre Moonlight Road property and—with his childhood friends—began a secret dogfighting operation disguised as a boarding and breeding kennel.

In 2003, Vick built a 4600 sq. ft., modern-style white brick home at the front of the property, complete with white iron fencing along the road and a basketball court behind. The house was impressive in an understated way, as if to say "this is but a small country retreat" for someone who had cash to spend and time to enjoy homes in various locations.

Yet, just half a football field to the rear of the home, the white fencing would transition to black, a physical manifestation of the darkness hidden behind the pristine facade. Tall trees and black paint served to camouflage the four cheaply-made—and quickly erected—sheds huddled within their branches.

It was in these sheds that the most nefarious activities took place.

While the majority of the dogs lived chained and scattered throughout the woodland acreage in the back, those selected to perform were brought to the sheds for training, forcible breeding, and—the ultimate goal of the compound—organized dog fights.

Those that failed to perform were killed.

By 2011, the house and property had stood vacant for four years.

After Vick's arrest, as it became more and more obvious the football star was in serious trouble, he quickly sold 1915 Moonlight Road on the down-low—cheap—to a local construction company by the name of Todd Builders. Ray Todd, president of the company, thought he could spruce up the place and do a quick turn-around due its famous owner, thereby making a financial killing.

The gambit didn't work out so well for him.

Todd Builders first put the home on the market in November of 2007, just a few months after purchase. The company had paid only $450,000 for a property worth more than $700,000, then dumped $50,000 into it to fix the floors, appliances, and walls. Todd tried to sell the property at auction—getting mostly lookie-loos—and failed to receive minimum asking price. Then he put it on the market for a cool million, where it stayed for six months before being dropped and then finally withdrawn.

Trouble was, Ray Todd didn't understand how tainted 1915

9

Moonlight Road, Smithfield, Virginia, had become. It turned out that no one wanted to buy the place where dogs were tortured, killed, and buried; no matter that the previous owner was a famous—now infamous—football player.

Todd Builders would be stuck with the property, reducing and raising the price as the market fluctuated, for the following four years.

The day was chilly but sunny, climbing into the 50's by mid-afternoon. As our small group toured the grounds, I was struck by a sense of the history here, and an urge to bring new life to this place of trauma was bubbling up inside me.

I could picture our dogs running the fields, snoozing in the house, peeing on the sheds. I could see it all.

Dogs Deserve Better's primary mission was to bring chained dogs into the home and family, which made the property an even more exciting fit for us: the dogs who suffered and lost their lives here had all lived chained, and then been forced to fight for survival too, adding injury to insult.

At 4600 square feet, the house itself was no mansion (as some would later claim), but would be a perfect size for a start-er facility for us and our dogs. It consisted of five bedrooms and 4.5 baths, plus a nice-sized entertainment room and two front entry rooms that I envisioned as office and meet and greet areas for visitors and our pups.

As I walked through the empty rooms, I never looked at it from the perspective of a homebuyer, but as a facility where we could house and train our rescue dogs for new and happier lives with a family, something they'd never experienced before. The land was flat and a bit depressing for my tastes—coming from the mountains of Pennsylvania—but I knew it wasn't about me: would the property and house work for the dogs?

The upstairs bedrooms would be perfect for live-in staff, overnight caretakers, and an office or two. A large entertainment room, complete with sink and mini-fridge, nestled at the top of the stairs between the bedrooms; I could imagine Vick's buds congregating there to drink, smoke pot, and watch him play ball, placing side bets on his performance.

To my mind, this same space would make an excellent break and conference room for the organization, or even a training and socialization area for our dogs. So many possibilities!

I became more and more excited about the potential for the property as we toured. The wooded acreage at the back had been cleared by Todd Builders in hopes of attracting horse fanciers, and I could readily envision a much-larger facility taking shape there, housing 50 dogs in small apartment-style condos where they would live with trainers and learn the ins and outs of becoming beloved family members.

I also wondered what would happen to the memories of those dogs if the place wasn't bought by someone who cared . . . would the sheds be leveled like the woods had been, the tragedy forgotten, glossed over, a blip on the radar screen of history? I didn't want that; those dogs deserved better, too.

Not only did I believe we could use what happened there as a cautionary tale—even making the sheds into a museum and memorial—if we owned the place, but I envisioned what the property could blossom into for our dogs and for our future as an organization. I felt the meaning behind the act.

By the end of the hour, I'd determined to buy the property.

Now, I just had to convince the other two board members that the idea could work, and raise a mere $595,000.

Easy peasy.

Me with my first ever rescue dog, Bo, formerly "Worthless"

CHAPTER TWO:

Who Were We to Buy this Property?

$\mathcal{J}$ had incorporated Dogs Deserve Better as a 501c3 nonprofit organization in 2002, when I founded and ran it out of my Bellwood, Pennsylvania, home.

At the time I was 38 years old, separated, and on my way to divorce; I was also floundering for a mission in life. I believed we humans were put on this earth with the potential to do something special, but I had no idea what my "something" could be.

I ran my own graphic design business from my small, split-level home on an acre in the countryside, and I co-habitated with my two children, two dogs, and two cats. I was unhappy with my lot in life, and wanted more . . . yes, material things would have been nice, but my soul called out for fulfillment. I was afraid of getting old, of dying without having made any kind of difference in the world.

I began searching for a mission, reading self-help books and asking the universe, or God if you will, for a purpose. There was one thing I did know for sure: I despised the act of dog chaining, and I'd been unfortunate enough to buy a home only ¼ mile from an old black lab named Worthless, who'd spent all of his 10+ years on a chain.

As I drove by his house each day—a reluctant witness to his suffering—I would mutter and swear to myself, utterings along the lines of "dogs deserve so much better than that." I'd complain and moan to myself and my kids, and then I'd call the humane society, who would tell me there was nothing they could do about it since it wasn't against the law. Repeat.

I was raised on a farm with a chained dog, a little beagle named Maggie, and her fate has haunted me ever since; I was shocked and fairly outraged that in the past 30 years this cruel treatment of our best friends had not ended. Was man not evolving at all?

Ask for a purpose and you shall receive one, it seems, even if it's way too difficult and you resist with all your might. Admittedly, I wasn't a fan of this proposed purpose, and argued with God about it. No way, no thank you. Was that really supposed to be on me? That seemed way too hard.

Too scary—I could get shot!

Who was I to tackle such a big problem by myself?

But the idea had lodged itself in my mind, and it pushed its annoying way to the forefront every time I passed sweet old Worthless, pacing on his chain in the rain, the sun, the snow, and the bitter cold.

Ugh. Watching him was torture.

Who was I *not* to tackle such a big problem?

I was being scared and selfish.

I decided I would do *something*, dip my toe into the issue, because at least that wasn't *nothing*. So I reluctantly started by designing and posting a "No Chains" sign in my van window, and spoke to friends and family about my feelings on the subject. The response I received was uniformly the same: "I agree with you, but there's nothing you can do about it. . . . you'll just get yourself hurt. . . . nothing will change, don't even bother . . ."

You see, at the time no one was taking on—or talking about— dog chaining. Not in any big or organized way at least. These dogs were what I would later call "the forgotten dogs." Because they had a home, but did they really? They were forgotten: alone, lonely, and miserable in America's backyards.

I had to face that fact that if I stood against chaining, I could very well be standing alone.

I finally decided I would stand alone.

By 2011 Dogs Deserve Better had grown to a national and widely-respected organization. We were the first to focus solely on dog chaining, harnessing an excitement around the issue and building an area rep base in states all over the U.S., even into other countries.

I was speaking at conferences about chained dogs, training others how to fight for laws and rescue dogs in their communities, and had garnered my share of activist arrests. I was most well-known for the open rescue of a dog named Doogie, an old shepherd mix who'd been left to die on his Pennsylvania chain.

When he could no longer stand and flailed about on the rain-soaked ground for three days, the neighbor became frantic to find help for him. After fruitless attempts on her part to get police and humane agents involved, DDB (myself and my assistant) agreed to go see the situation for ourselves.

When we pulled up to the address, Doogie was lying immobile on the wet ground in the rain, and I thought we were too late. Was he dead? But as we walked closer, he lifted his head and looked at me, as if to say "will YOU help me?" *

How could I not?

So we picked him up, carried him to our van, and raced to the vet. The local humane officer had finally responded, and was waiting for us as we arrived at the vet's office. He could see that Doogie was unable to stand, toted him inside for us, and then proceeded to lecture me about "stealing" the dog.

"If you want to help him instead of me, please, be my guest," I told him, motioning with my hand. "In fact, I'll put him back on the chain right now if you promise to pick him up and get him the care he deserves."

He demurred, but pledged to take out a warrant for cruelty against the owner through legal channels. That never happened; instead, he informed the police I'd taken the dog, and within

---
* Video at https://bit.ly/2p1h937

hours the East Freedom police were calling me. By that evening I'd been ordered to return the dog or face arrest myself.

I refused. How could I in good conscience live with myself were I to return this poor wretched creature to the chain and the people who left him there to die?

No. Just no.

That night I was arrested for theft and receiving stolen property, hauled off in the back of a paddy wagon to the magistrate's office, arraigned, and dumped onto the street at 2:00 a.m.—with no money or ID.

I sent Doogie away before the police arrived, and moved him a couple of times until he'd found a safe place to rest his weary head. He spent the remaining six months of his life with a rescuer I respected and trusted, someone who to this day prefers to be anonymous. Good food, vet care, and proper medications brought him as close to health as his old age would permit, helping to manage his painful back spurs and get him back on his feet. Soon, he was able to walk, and even trotted to his foster mom looking for attention and treats.*

A year later, ironically around the same time that Vick was being sentenced by the feds for dogfighting, I was convicted and sentenced to 300 hours of community service for a "people organization", because—according to the judge—"people are dogs, too."

But . . . but . . . aren't most dogs nicer than humans?

Doogie's life was worth it to me, and I never once regretted what I endured for helping him. Seeing him fill out, his fur become shiny, learning that he would eventually run again? Incredible.

Dogs Deserve Better, rescuing chained dogs, had become my purpose, and I'd finally found a mission in life that mattered to someone, even if it wasn't appreciated by those in power and control.

It mattered to the dogs.

2011 was our ninth year in business as a nonprofit, and we'd begun to dream about our own facility to train and care for formerly chained dogs. In fiscal year 2010, the organization had brought in $265,000 in donations, and I was paid full-time as CEO of the company, making a whopping $32,000 per year.

From 2005-2010, we'd raised over a million dollars for the cause. While that's small potatoes compared to many of the larger nonprofits, for us it was a huge amount given that we'd started with nothing; it was time we had a place to call our own.

I'd fostered dogs out of my home since my first rescue, Worthless, who you might remember as the dog who inspired me to take action for him and all those living as he was. His caretaker had finally relented, saying "just take him, my daughter doesn't feed him anyway."

I would quickly learn that I had no idea how to teach a dog

---

* Video at https://bit.ly/2Ph6ZGf

to live inside the home with the family—as chained dogs weren't housetrained, people trained, or trained to get along with other animals. The males would ultimately prove more difficult than the females, since they were inclined to lift their leg to mark territory—everywhere! These newly-unchained dogs gave a whole new and equally gruesome meaning to the term "golden showers."

By the time I visited Vick's property that February day in 2011, I'd fostered in the neighborhood of 250 dogs from my home, 4-6 at a time, and I was ready—ready for them to move out and get a place of their own, and ready to get my own home back to a more peaceful and livable condition.

In those days, the organization had an active yahoo discussion board (remember those?) for our area reps, and we often dreamed and brainstormed about buying property to build our own center. One of the area reps from the western side of Virginia, Shannon Allen, posted the following email to the group on January 27, 2011:

Subject: Great Location For DDB Rehab Center and Rescue

"This is Michael Vick's [former] house which was originally listed at $1.1 mil, now down to $600,000. The house is on a pretty vacant road, 15 acres (mostly wooded), and fenced. I know Vick doesn't own the house anymore (the bank took it [untrue]) but how cool would it be to get it donated. Or we could start a Chip In :).

"Before you think I am crazy and twisted, take a look! This would make a GREAT rescue/rehab!! We could call it Dogs Deserve Better's Good Newz Rehabilitation Center, since Vick's kennel was called Bad Newz."

Just four days after Shannon's suggestion and the resultant stir it caused amongst the reps (mostly favorable), Monica and I would arrive onsite to tour the property.

The front window with the bullet hole. I thought the glass was supposed to look like that.

CHAPTER THREE:

Fundraising

"AN ANIMAL RIGHTS GROUP IS TRYING TO BUY MICHAEL VICK'S FORMER HOME TO TURN IT INTO AN ANIMAL REHAB CENTER. BECAUSE THAT'S JUST WHAT ABUSED ANIMALS WANT TO HEAR: 'IT'S GOING TO BE OKAY—YOU'RE GOING TO MICHAEL VICK'S HOUSE!'"—CONAN O'BRIEN, FEBRUARY 08, 2011

*D*eb Carr, DDB Treasurer, and Tracy Copes, DDB Secretary, were easily won over on the proposal to buy 1915 Moonlight Road, even though I was admittedly nervous about making the pitch—would they think I was insane? Would they stand against the idea? Instead, it seemed that the excitement about what the property offered and what we could do there was infectious.

They loved that the house was large enough for staff to stay onsite with the dogs, and that we'd immediately have room to work with more rescued dogs, too—with lots of acreage for future growth.

Plus, the idea of "taking over" Vick's dogfighting compound? Priceless.

It was a BIG, BOLD move, but that was DDB's modus operandi in those days . . . we went big or we went home.

We'd decided to go big.

I would have a lot to learn about getting a facility off the ground, and my first lesson was that we couldn't start fundraising until we put a 45-day contract on the property. After all, if we started raising the money without a hold on the place, someone else could all too easily swoop in and plunk down the $595,000 while we were still out begging like amateurs.

The contract required a $5,000 downpayment, though, which we would lose if we weren't able to come up with the funds in time. I gulped.

$5,000 was a LOT of money to our organization! I bit my lip but made the leap, aware I was committing to something that terrified me: raising over half a million dollars in 45 days? How in the world were we, was I, going to accomplish THAT?

As it turns out, not very well.

Dogs Deserve Better had saved $40,000 toward the purchase of a facility, and in the first 20 days we would raise another

$60,000 dollars, for a total of approximately $100,000. But we still needed another $500,000 in order to buy the home and 15 acres!

We'd gotten creative with it, taking a "vote" online as a fundraiser that cost $1.00 per vote and asking the question: should we buy the Vick dogfighting compound and reboot it, or put the money toward another piece of property and build instead? We hoped we could raise a good portion of the funds from the vote alone, assuming that dog lovers would want us to know how they felt, positively or negatively.

Fail.

What donors we did attract overwhelmingly voted for us to choose the Vick place, and most seemed to share in our wave of excitement. There were some folks who were just plain disgusted by the place and wanted it burned to the ground—which I got, and I could honor those feelings, too.

We'd also alerted the media immediately after getting a contract in place, hoping to get the word out about our plans and funds coming in, but—as is often the case—this quickly turned into a double-edged sword. Many folks who hadn't know about our work for chained dogs loved the idea and gave a few dollars to the cause, but there were plenty of people posting negative comments, as well as blog posts and articles falsely claiming we had failed in our efforts to raise the money.

This kind of negative publicity caused some potential donors to back away, and we were constantly put in the position of having to reassure our supporters that we were moving forward despite what they were reading online.

AMENDMENT / ADDENDUM TO PURCHASE AGREEMENT   REIN

This document forms an integral part of the Purchase Agreement ("Agreement") dated _____ 02/01/11 _____

between _____ DOGS   DESERVE BETTER INC. , _____ ("Buyer")
and _____ TODD   BUILDERS INC   . _____ ("Seller")
and _____ Long & Foster REALTORS _____ ("Selling Firm")
and _____ LONG & FOSTER REALTORS _____ ("Listing Firm")
for all that certain piece, parcel or lot of land described as follows to-wit: _____
_____ 1915 MOONLIGHT ROAD   SMITHFIELD , VA 23430 _____

_____ ("Property").

The undersigned Buyer and Seller hereby agree to the following:

  1) CLOSING DATE TO BE ON OR BEFORE MAY 31, 2011

In the end, it took us two 30-day extensions and two loans, but we would close on the home and property at 1915 Moonlight Road, Smithfield, Virginia, almost five months later and with $179,431.66 in hand. We would owe a mortgage debt to Fulton Bank for $297,500, and the current property owners—Todd Builders—a secondary mortgage of $119,000 based on the same terms and interest.

Dogs Deserve Better Inc. was slated to be the new (and proud?) owners of Vick's former dogfighting compound, Bad Newz Kennels.

I breathed a sigh of relief, thinking that the hardest part was behind me. Boy, I never knew I could be so very wrong.

My foster dog Sloan peeks over the table at the loan signing.

CHAPTER FOUR:

Closing Day

C losing was set for 1:00 p.m. May 27, 2011, a warm, sunny day, at the lawyer's high-rise office in Virginia Beach, Virginia. Monica, who'd been a big part of our fundraising team and donated a portion of the money, was on hand, as well as our realtor, the lawyers, and a Hampton Roads Magazine reporter and photographer.

My fiancé, Joe, and I drove down from his apartment in northern Virginia that morning, bringing with us one of my DDB foster dogs, Sloan. Sloan was a shepherd who would add his "stamp" of approval to the acquisition, and garner the dubious honor of being the first dog to—legally at least—step foot on the property where dogs fought and died since the 2007 seizure of Vick's 66 remaining dogs.

Sloan had been rescued just that winter from his Pennsylvania chain, and had been living with me as a foster dog for the last six months. Although I wished he could talk, could tell me how he ended up in that awful situation, I grew to believe he hadn't spent his whole life that way: he was both neutered AND housetrained, a rarity in my world.

Believing this almost made me pity him *more* than the other dogs I'd rescued—because those poor pups didn't know what they were missing . . . but a dog who'd been part of a family at one time? His life on the chain would be even more miserable, because he'd understand and mourn both his lack of freedom and the family who'd abandoned him.

On our way to the signing, we stopped at 1915 Moonlight Road for a final walk-through before purchase. In a bit of last-minute drama, a storm had blown through since we'd last been there, and a branch had impaled one of the shed roofs, tearing it up in a couple spots and embedding itself into the structure. We wanted a promise from Todd Builders that they'd fix the roof since it happened on their watch, and our insurance wouldn't cover it as we didn't own the property when it happened. But Ray Todd refused, and so we had to make a hasty decision as to whether to walk away from the buy or not. In the end, the two realtors offered to split the cost of the fix out of their proceeds so the signing would go through.

We accepted, with reluctance. Todd Builders could have easily and quickly sent a team out to the property to fix the roof, accepting the responsibility that by all rights was theirs. Their refusal was irksome to me, but I also didn't want to disappoint our donors who were counting on us to close on the property. So we moved forward, and the deal was back on track.

I was justifiably nervous about the financial obligations I was committing to on behalf of the organization, and my palms were sweaty as I sat down to look over and sign the purchase paperwork. Joe and I were both on the hook as personal backers for the loans, too, which meant that if the organization failed to make the payments down the road, we'd become liable ourselves. Scary stuff!

Monica had pledged to donate $5,000 a month for the next ten years, which would cover our mortgage payments plus some. The pledge came with no written guarantee, however, just a verbal assurance—yet another thing that should have been enough to give me pause.

Sloan's presence calmed me and reminded me that he and others like him needed a safe place to rest their heads; he reminded me why I was there. All eyes were on him as he played the part of the well-behaved gentleman to a T, even giving his pawprint of approval and hamming it up for the photographers.

Before we knew it, and after months of work and worry, Dogs Deserve Better was now the official new owner of Michael Vick's dogfighting compound in Surry County, Virginia! A cheer went up amongst the dozen or so folks in the room, and I was ecstatic but also terrified.

What had I done?

Having never been inside a high-rise before, Sloan was so over-stimulated by all the new experiences and emotions that he ran right into the glass doors as we exited the elevators, looking about in confusion as if to say, "What sorcery is this?"

Keys in hand, we drove to the property for a celebration with office manager Elaine P., her daughter Kali, and Sloan, where we filmed our rescue boy entering his new home for the first time.* With the exception of a missed turn at the doorway,

---

* See the video here: https://bit.ly/2lXG45U

our pup rose to the challenge like a champ, giving the place his wag of approval before laying down and getting in a quick nap. The day's ordeal had plum tuckered him out.

As we'd pulled into our organization's new home for the second time that day, we were sobered by the fact that our neighbor had installed not just one, but a whole row of "No Trespassing" signs along the left side of the front yard, in a not so subtle "You're not welcome here" message.

Were we to have trouble already, before we even officially moved to the property? It would seem that way.

I felt hurt and confused: why would a neighbor have no problem with a dogfighter and more than 50 chained and barking dogs next door, but would immediately go after a non-profit whose only goal was to help dogs out of these same living conditions?

It would be the first of many hard lessons calling out my naivete.

We spent an hour onsite, popping the cork on a bottle of champagne and exploring the new digs, and then we packed up and drove back to Joe's northern Virginia apartment, trying not to let the down sides of the day ruin the good: we'd bought a home for our rescue dogs, AND taken over the site of horrific animal abuse.

It was a win for the good guys, even if it wasn't viewed that way by everyone.

Sloan surveys the dogs' new "kingdom", and dreams about our big center with me.

Chain Off 2011 at the Pennsylvania State Capitol. Photo by Redheaded Ninja.

CHAPTER FIVE:

Chain Off and A Doghouse Wedding

$\mathcal{E}$very morning we get to experience the gift of FREEDOM. As humans, we have choices, even when we feel that only one of them is viable—such as getting up and going to work. Each day brings with it a fresh start, a new opportunity to choose kindness over anger, love over hate, right over moral wrong.

But the chained dogs don't have a choice without us. They don't get to experience FREEDOM as you and I know it, and their choices are limited to finding a spot in which to lay that isn't covered in feces. Snow, rain? Forget about it! **They don't get the chance to run, to play, to cuddle, to know human love.**

And, most importantly, they don't have the voice to say "I DON'T WANT TO LIVE THIS WAY ANYMORE. Please stop."

We have to be this voice for them.

That's what Chain Off was all about for me. **We put ourselves into the paws of these helpless beings for a day in order to advocate for them, to spread the word that chaining doesn't cut it, and encourage social change and better laws for Man's Best Friend.**

There were two things on the agenda before we could move the organization from my Bellwood, Pennsylvania, home to the Smithfield, Virginia, property: the DDB 2011 Chain Off, and my Doghouse Wedding.

I'd wisely combined the two into one all-day event taking place Monday, June 20th—just three weeks away, and now that we'd closed on the center, I needed to focus my attention elsewhere.

My friend Gordon Bakalar, chained and inside his doghouse.

Dogs Deserve Better had been holding Chain Off events every summer since 2004, and along the way I'd—unbelievably and inexplicably—convinced others to chain up with me to advocate for the voiceless in spots all around the country. The first year I chained myself to a doghouse in the college home of Penn State University for 33 hours—in pantyhose and business skirt no less—then varied that theme throughout the years, even spending 54 days chained to a doghouse in front of the Pennsylvania state Capitol in Harrisburg, Pennsylvania, in 2010 advocating for passage of a law.[*]

(Yes, I failed, and no, I didn't sleep there. I spent 8 a.m.-6 p.m. Monday-Friday chained to my doghouse until the bill died in committee.)

But this year I wanted MORE people to show up at the Pennsylvania Capitol building and chain with me. I wanted lawmakers to know we weren't going away, that the dogs were still not free. But how could I create higher interest?

Well, I WAS engaged: What about a Doghouse Wedding? *After all, what woman can't be enticed into just about anything by the allure of a good wedding?*

I'd always wanted to be married in an unusual way. This would be my fourth marriage (I never claimed to be good at it) so I'd already done the traditional wedding thing. Twice.

As I sat for days on end staring at the Capitol building during my campaign the previous summer through fall—mostly bored out of my mind like every chained dog—it became all too easy to picture a fancy Doghouse Wedding on those very Capitol steps. It was a gorgeous backdrop.

What cooler way to combine raising awareness for an important cause AND getting hitched?

Trouble was, my intended, Joe—a fellow Air Force veteran I'd served with many moons ago in Germany—wasn't feelin' the same overwhelming sense of rightness about it that I was. As an introvert, the very thought of being chained to a doghouse in a tuxedo—in front of a bunch of people and in a very public

---

[*] Find links to my book about the experience, *Capitol in Chains*, at www.whochainsyou.com.

place—freaked him out. He gently, but resolutely, refused my plea for a Doghouse Wedding.

I was terribly saddened and disappointed about it, even though I understood his feelings. He tried talking me into other, more traditional, avenues like a destination or beach wedding, but my heart just wasn't in it.

I also knew I couldn't make my—admittedly weird—dream his too. And I didn't know how to fix the situation.

I really thought Joe was "the one." After 45 years, I'd met the man who truly felt like HOME to me; the man who loved but didn't baby me, and let me go into crazy or potentially dangerous situations in rescue and activist work without trying to scare or shame me out of it.

He respected me as an equal partner, and didn't overprotect or control, as many men would have done in his shoes. He got me, even though we were very different people at this stage of our lives.

I wasn't willing to relinquish my dream of getting married chained to a doghouse, and he wasn't willing to relinquish his notion of getting married in a more traditional fashion.

We were at an impasse.

We went about our daily lives, Joe living and working in Virginia, and me working for the chained dogs from my home in Pennsylvania. We were still engaged, and continued to spend time together as much as we possibly could.

We skirted the subject for the next four months, but I nonetheless started planning a Chain Off event for the Pennsylvania Capitol steps that June. As we discussed summer plans, I jokingly said to him, "Well, we'd better get your tux ordered then. We're running out of time."

He said, "Yeah, I guess you're right. Let's do it." I was floored! Now, mind you, he still wasn't jumping for joy about it, but he had agreed to the idea, and that meant a lot.

I was beyond ecstatic. "Are you sure?" I asked; I was afraid to get my hopes up and then have him back out.

"Yes, I'm sure, honey," he hugged me, looking me in the eye. "I love you, and I want you to be happy. If this is what it takes, then sign me up."

I grinned for a week. I don't even consider myself a girly girl, but if I had a chance to stand up for the animals AND watch an animal activist wedding at the end of the day? Count me in.

I immediately announced that the wedding would take place at 5:00 p.m. at the end of Chain Off in Harrisburg, Pennsylvania, and all our DDB supporters—plus friends and family, of course— were invited . . .

Our list of event participants, aka chainees, immediately doubled! (It was one of my more brilliant moves.)

That Monday dawned hot and sunny, and there were 40 bodies and 40 doghouses splashed all over the Capitol steps; we would certainly not to be ignored today! The wedding "prize" at the end of a long, sweaty event got started late, but in the end it exceeded my expectations, and was even filmed by a local news crew who put it on their website. It was so amazing, I'd do it all over again if I could—and do it even better the second time!

Our Doghouse Wedding. Photo by Redheaded Ninja.

The most memorable part of the wedding was the "blooper reel." First, I tripped on my gown going down the steps, but luckily Joe caught me so I didn't end up face planted and on my way to the hospital instead of the honeymoon suite.

Then Mark—our Air Force friend who was performing the ceremony for us—had forgotten to print out new vows, and was using a script from a previous wedding he'd performed. When it came time for Joe's vows, he mistakenly called him Scott, the name of the previous groom. "Do you Scott, take . . . "

I immediately cracked up laughing, and without missing a beat, Joe turned and looked around at the wedding guests, calling out "Scott? Scott?" I still smile today when I remember that moment.

I wouldn't doubt that there are now times he wishes there had been a Scott around to take me off his hands!

Joe's joke about the doghouse wedding has been the same since the day he said "I'll do it."

"A guy starting his marriage off in the doghouse . . . surely he can only move up from there? . . ."

Volunteers in Florida chain up on behalf of the dogs.

Nationally that year we would end up with 81 people chaining themselves to doghouses in 18 states, including Arizona, California, Connecticut, Florida, Illinois, Iowa, Maryland, Michigan, Minnesota, Missouri, New Mexico, New York, Pennsylvania, Tennessee, Washington, West Virginia, Wisconsin, Wyoming, and Guam.

Volunteer Diana Bevensee installs the mailbox.

CHAPTER SIX:

Moving In

That weekend, June 25th, Joe captained the U-Haul, I drove the van I shared with the organization, and office manager Elaine P. piloted her SUV the 350 miles to what would now officially be known as the "DDB Good Newz Rehab Center for Chained and Penned Dogs".

We brought with us eight dogs—my six fosters and Elaine's two personal companions—plus my three cats and Elaine's teenage daughter. The six-hour+ trip went as well as you could expect—as long as you expected a gray cat named Tuna to let loose with a massive doody in the carrier and slather himself and two other cats in some really noxious feces. Tuna's action

35

IT WENT TO THE DOGS

quickly engendered an equal and opposite reaction in me, of the "I'm gonna' hurl" variety, followed by a frantic call for cleanup aid to the man driving the U-Haul and a disgruntled wipedown of cats and carrier in a shopping center parking lot. Ah, good times.

Elaine had been with Dogs Deserve Better since earlier that year, and worked from my Pennsylvania home with me in all aspects of the organization, to include basic bookkeeping, dog care, and front office work. She was eager to move to Virginia with the organization to start a new adventure, and our plan was that both she and I would live onsite while we got it off the ground, and then we'd reassess down the line.

The place was plenty big enough for both of us. Elaine and Kali would take the two bedrooms to the right of the upstairs hallway, sharing a bathroom. I would be living at the other end of the house, in the bigger of the two master bedrooms, which had most certainly been designed and reserved for Vick and Vick alone.

I'd hazard a guess that the master bedroom and adjoining bath and walk-in closet went at least 800 sq. ft., the size of the whole upstairs of my Pennsylvania home. There was an oversized Jacuzzi tub, as well as a walk-in shower, and a separate "chute" for the toilet and a door for a little privacy during "go time".

From the first of my many experiences with Vick's toilet, two things immediately stood out, which you'll promptly thank me for knowing: 1.) I consistently tried and failed miserably to NOT picture Vick's butt sitting in the exact same spot as mine—you're welcome for the mental imagery, on both counts. In fact, the more I tried to mentally unsee it, the more it happened and I couldn't get around the fact that I used the same toilet as a confessed—yet famous—serial (animal) killer; and 2.) The toilet was crooked, and leaned to the left, engendering even more discomfort in what should be a peaceful moment. A pro football player with a crooked toilet? Now I'd seen it all.

I would sometimes lapse into pondering the depths of the meaning behind that crooked toilet. Was "crooked" a metaphor for what was going on in the back of the house?

Maybe I was overthinking.
On all counts.

Volunteers are interviewed by TV crews.

Our first full day onsite was extremely busy, with media coming to interview us and at least ten volunteers showing up to help unload the truck. We were well-aware that most of the folks coming to carry boxes just wanted a look at the place, and who could blame them: Vick's case was probably THE most famous animal abuse case in history. We were still incredibly grateful for the help, and knew a little curiosity was only natural and human.

In fact, we were hoping that human curiosity would bring even more volunteers as time went on, and they'd like it so much they'd keep coming back.

They say if you can't take the heat, get out of the kitchen. But what if you're too dumb to know the kitchen is hot, and so you just breeze on in like you own the joint?

If only I'd understood then that Tuna's doody might have been the bright spot of my move to Virginia, I might have been able to appreciate it.

No, not even then.

Sloan resting in the yard on the day we closed. Ferguson Grove Baptist Church, behind.

CHAPTER SEVEN:

My Naivete and Racial Tensions in the County

"WHAT IN THE WORLD IS GOING ON IN SURRY COUNTY? THIS CERTAINLY DOESN'T MAKE ME FEEL WARM AND FUZZY ABOUT THE SURRY COUNTY ATTORNEY."—KATHY STROUSE, ANIMAL CONTROL OFFICER, REGARDING THE VICK CASE

I never thought of myself as a naïve person, but looking back now I can see that I absolutely had been. Before arriving onsite, there were beliefs I held that I'd never questioned the rightness of: that chaining dogs for life and forcing them to fight was wrong, and that buying Vick's property was a morally strong countermove in answer to both of those abuses.

As a result, I firmly believed that because DDB was doing good and helping dogs, we would be embraced and welcomed by the community of Surry County, Virginia.

Wrong.

I mistakenly assumed that the citizens and leadership of Surry County would feel a collective sense of shame about Vick's activities—which had taken place right under their noses, after all—and would want to support the nonprofit moving in, as a way to gain back their county's reputation and sense of well-being.

Wrong.

I unwisely thought that they would be proud to have us there, to show the world, "Look, Vick was not who we are."

Wrong, wrong, wrong.

I wonder now how I could have been so blind.

Remember how I told you for the full story you'd need to read *The Lost Dogs* and *Badd Newz*? I myself hadn't followed that advice, and had read neither book before buying and moving to the property. When I finally made the time to dive into them as I searched for answers to what was happening to us, not only was I blown away by the level of corruption in the county, but I understood so much more about what I was up against.

Oh, and I was a dumbass.

I recently ran across a quote by a political writer named Robert Harrison, and it fit the mistakes I'd made to a T: "It's better to be cautious and wrong than incautious and caught by surprise."

I had naively assumed we'd be widely accepted, even celebrated for turning something bad into something good. What's not to love about rescuing dogs? But had I been wise enough to read the books before sauntering into that kitchen fire, I'd like to think I'd also have been wise enough to never open the door.

Hindsight is always too late to fix the problem.

It seemed, among other things, I'd stumbled my way into a low-roiling race war. And I was now just another pawn.

I tended to always side with the underdog, but in this case, due to the color of my skin, I landed on the white team without even being asked. There's about half of the white team that I really dislike, though (especially these days), and many of them chain their dogs and do other repugnant things like discriminate based on color, sex, sexual preference, etc.

I like to maintain that I'm kinda yellowish, and as proof I offer this conversation I once had with a Korean woman at a nail salon.

Her: "Where you from?"

Me: "Pennsylvania."

Her: "No, where you from?"

Me, baffled: "Penn-syl-va-nia." [Said a littler slower and louder . . . maybe she didn't hear me?]

Her, equally baffled now: "You mean you're not Korean?"

Me, laughing: "No . . . not unless my mother slept with the mailman, which my father has been known to claim."

Alas, DNA testing from both 23andMe and Ancestry.com show that I am almost wholly of Western European ancestry, and am indeed the biological child of the man my mother married. It's unfortunate. This makes me, genetically speaking at least, a boring old white supremacist's wet dream. Gross.

I was by no means interested in landing in a race war; I'm a firm believer in equality for ALL, but apparently I had no choice in the matter. I bought Vick's house, and so the war came to me.

Three facts need to be made clear before there is any discussion of race in our purchase of the property:

1. Vick did not commit crimes against the animals I stood for because he was black.

2. I did not buy Vick's property because of his skin color, but because he committed crimes against the animals I stood for.

3. I would also have bought the property if Vick had been white and committed the same crimes.

That seems to be a pretty open and shut case of cause and effect, no? And skin color played no part in it.

But, as luck would have it, the accusations would be made anyway.

Surry County, Virginia is a largely flat, rural county, bordering the James River in the Hampton Roads area of the state. The population sits at under 7,000, of which approximately 52% are white and 45% are black. When we moved in, the majority of leadership in the county was black, which one might have thought was a good thing given all the corruption occurring in white leadership these days. In truth, whether leadership is black, brown, yellow, or white, every person in the county should be treated the same; when power is used to discriminate against citizens who have a different skin tone than leadership, then there's a problem no matter which "color" is in control.

Right after we moved onto the property, Wayne Coffey of the *New York Daily News* wrote a lengthy article about us. In that article, an "anonymous source" was quoted as saying there was "an unmistakable racial underbelly to the matter, with a white woman charging into town on the proverbial white horse to clean up the criminal misdeeds of young black men, among them an iconic figure in this part of Virginia."

I'd wager a guess, without proof mind you—other than the fact that he'd used the word "icon" multiple times when discussing Vick—that the quote came from none other than then-Commonwealth Attorney Gerald Poindexter, who happens to be a black man. Poindexter's behavior during the Vick debacle had raised a lot of eyebrows, and his focus on race made local sheriff Bill Brinkman and federal agent Jim Knorr extremely uncomfortable when working the Vick case, according to *The Lost Dogs*.

Brinkman told the Virginian Pilot: "Every time you met with him, it was a very unsettling, uncomfortable, degrading conversation. Everything's wrapped around race."

I would learn from locals that even though there was close

to a 50/50 split in race in the county, the two races didn't get along with one another, and as a result they either ignored each other or fought amongst themselves.

Across the street from our property was a small white church with a largely black congregation, called the Ferguson Grove Baptist Church.

On February 8th, very shortly after we announced our quest to buy the Vick property, we got the following e-mail:

> "I see in the Virginian-Pilot that it is your intentions to place a dog pound across the road and directly in front of my place of worship. This is notice that I plan to take every action necessary to see that this does not happen. If you want this activity, put it next to or across the street from your house of worship. Our house of worship has a long and historic past and I don't plan to see it diminished by the noise of dog yelps, poop, etc.
>
> "I am quite certain you would not have proposed such in front of a house of worship of predominantly White congregants, so don't propose to do so at our front door because we are a church of Black worshippers."
>
> *Wallace D. Johnson, Jr.*
> *Surry & Norfolk, Virginia*

Had I been paying attention, this would have given me pause as to the kind of shitstorm I'd be walking into, but I dismissed it as a one-off and went about my business.

Confirming my errant thoughts, we shortly thereafter got a nice email from a deacon of the church, letting us know that wasn't the official position of the church.

> "I am Deacon Herbert Blount with the Ferguson Grove Baptist Church Deacon Ministry. Last week you received an email from one of our church members. I

want to advise you and your staff that in no way this individual was speaking on behalf of the Ferguson Grove Baptist Church family.

"While this individual was entitled to their own opinion, their comments were not the voice of our church. I have attached a copy of the word document that was sent to Virginian Pilot Reporter, Linda McNatt. In that memo, we clearly demonstrated that this individual acted on their own behalf and not as a spokesperson or a representative for the Ferguson Grove Baptist Church."

Thank you for your understanding
and May God Bless you,
Ferguson Grove Baptist Church Deacon Ministry

While Mr. Johnson would not succeed in depriving us of our right to purchase property in the county, to my knowledge the church never overtly caused us problems after that day. Once we arrived at 1915 Moonlight Road, the parishioners pretended like we didn't exist, not even waving when they saw us outside. I'm not sure that's the most Christian of attitudes, but I'd take it any day of the week over out and out aggression.

If you can't treat those who are trying to make a difference with kindness, at least do them the courtesy of ignoring them.

In pondering the dilemma, I would often wonder: if I were racist to buy the property next to the church, didn't that make Vick racist too? After all, I only ended up there because Vick had chosen that spot first.

The irony of Mr. Johnson having no problem at all with Michael Vick and his 66 chained—and fought, and slaughtered— dogs living across from their church but having a problem with our dogs—who would all live inside the home—speaks more to his own prejudice along racial lines than anything I had said or done.

I can guarantee you that Vick never got such an email.

I was, and still am, of the opinion that any neighbor who condoned Michael Vick's actions had no right to complain about our well-cared-for dogs living onsite. I found the unfairness of such allegations intolerable.

I think a more logical point could be made that both Vick and DDB (aka me) behaved boorishly through the act of putting barking dogs next to a church that catered to any skin color.

At least that was an argument with merit.

Even though the detractors hit hardest, loudest, and longest, that doesn't mean there was no local support for us. Unfortunately, controversy is more likely to grab the attention of the media and linger longer in the minds of the people being attacked.

I know there was at least one supporter on our same road, because around the same time we got the following email:

> "I live in Surry County on Moonlight Road. I am sending this to you to let you know that I am interested in helping out. . . . I think this a GREAT THING so please feel free to call me."

Dog collar left in the fighting shed. Photo by Rita Thomas.

Our very first fence, just big enough to let the dogs out in shifts to do their business.

CHAPTER EIGHT:

Building Fences, and Mending None

*M*y plot in Pennsylvania was only an acre in size, but on that lot I'd installed two fences with doggie doors for my foster dogs, so they could be separated as necessary but still have access to the great outdoors to explore, play, and do their business.

When we arrived at 1915 Moonlight Road, the only fencing onsite was the white iron decorative one running along the road; there was nothing enclosed and we had eight dogs to somehow get exercised and given the bathroom breaks they needed.

We found ourselves leash-walking incessantly, and it was a miserable turn of events. I'd forgotten the beauty of a secure fence, and installing even a tiny area just for potty breaks became priority #1.

Removing the basketball hoops for transport to their new home.

The hoops reinstalled in a Virginia Beach community center.

Quickly—within a matter of weeks—our fencing would swell to encompass the basketball court directly behind the house. DDB had no use for expensive basketball hoops in caring for our dogs, so we decided they should make a difference in the lives of area youth. In the spirit of cooperation, we offered the hoops—valued at over $3000—to Surry County Parks and Recreations. Our outreach was ignored.

The hoops ended up finding a great home anyway, going to a community recreational facility in Virginia Beach, where they installed a small placard nearby thanking DDB for the donation.

In stages, with multiple fencing parties and the efforts of many wonderful volunteers, the fencing at the Good Newz Rehab Center gradually expanded outward; six months later, by January of 2012, approximately half of the 15-acre property was completely enclosed.

The dogs were finally free to experience the joy of off-leash antics twice a day! Our rescue pups renewed delight in the business of living reminded us what truly mattered, and you'll see many photos of them running the fields gracing the pages of this book.

Larry Oxton trains another volunteer how to install fencing. Sloan snoopervises.

Dogs at play after the initial fence is finished.

Three fenced dog yards for separation as needed.

Dogs loving their donated bone pools.

Fencing moves out to the field for a large running area.

The very last push for 7.5 acres fenced!

Dogs run in the first snowfall.

My son Rayne and his best friend Christian work on the fence after basic training.

The dogs dearly loved their runs twice a day!

Meanwhile, not long after we'd arrived onsite, we were summoned to a meeting with the county, during which they asked us what our intentions were with the property.

As a commercial kennel license was by-right in Surry County, Virginia, I hadn't thought any kind of permission from local authorities was needed to go about our business. The county is zoned agricultural/rural, which largely meant anything outside these two designations that they didn't want would be prohibited from setting up shop there. But a by-right designation means you don't have to apply for any special permits or worry about being turned away. Silly me.

In Permitted Uses in the county, section 13 specifies: Dog kennels, commercial or non-commercial are permitted; provided any open pens, runs, cages or kennels shall be located at least 200 feet from any side or rear lot lines.

That was it.

Piece of cake for us, since our dogs lived inside the home. We would have no open pens, runs, kennels, or cages. I patted myself on the back. I was gonna ACE this county test.

When I told them we hoped to—at some point—build to house 50 dogs onsite, they took that in stride. But when they found out our "commercial kennel" would need an office space too? Look. Out!

We would need an exception! A very special exception! There would have to be a vote on this at a public meeting!

But . . . I was confused. Wouldn't any commercial kennel have an office component to the business? How are they to keep records of sales and all aspects of running a company without employees and an office?

Oh, and as an aside, we wanted to sell a very small selection of our books and t-shirts from the office space if volunteers or donors who stopped by wanted to purchase any.

A store front! No WAY! Look. Out!

We needed an exception! A very special exception! There would have to be a vote on this at a public meeting!

Things had quickly taken a nosedive. It seemed we were allowed by right to keep dogs in poor conditions like Vick had, but running a commercial kennel in a manner that treated the dogs as companions and not commodities caused them to balk. Needless to say, I was horrified at whatever seemed to be taking place here.

They told me they'd be in touch, and then sent a notice to appear at a 6:00 Meeting of the Zoning Board on Wednesday, August 17, 2011.

I wondered if I should hire an attorney, but the one I e-mailed with wanted to charge $3000 to come there to represent us.

We were cash poor, had a mortgage to pay, and needed so much for the property. Spending $3000 to defend ourselves against whatever the county was cooking up was just not in the cards. It looked like I was on my own. How hard could it be?

I was clueless about the ambush awaiting me.

The neighbor with the myriad "No Trespassing" signs, Richard Clark, had—surprise surprise—created a petition to get rid of us, on which he'd garnered a whopping 64 signatures. He stood and presented them, along with comments about how we would disrupt the community.

The neighbor to the other side, Mr. Hardy, stood and complained about the time our dog Ebby escaped her leash, and Elaine crossed onto his property to retrieve her. Meanwhile, Mr. Hardy's dogs ran loose up and down the road and around the neighborhood on a daily basis!

By the end of the "meeting", aka smear fest, I was in tears and left the room. One of the zoning board members, a woman whose name I no longer remember, came out and told me to buck up, that I'd need to get a much thicker skin if I were going to survive this. She was right. I was so embarrassed that I'd lost it in there, but I wasn't emotionally prepared to be attacked like that.

It reminded me of when I was a teenager, and my father would come home from his high school teaching job, angry and full of hatred for his work, his bosses, and his pupils. He'd find some reason to take it out on his own children at the dinner table each night, calling us names and demeaning us. I'd often been blindsided by the attacks, and there were numerous times

I'd get up and run from the table in tears.

I'd been through my share of woes in fighting for the rights of the chained dogs, but this felt like getting destroyed for simply existing. It was not a good feeling.

By the time I was allowed to speak, I was shaky as I read my prepared statement to the county:

DEAR SURRY COUNTY CITIZENS:

As you're all aware, our organization has bought the property at 1915 Moonlight Road, Smithfield, Virginia, and we are transforming it to the Good Newz Rehab Center for Chained and Penned Dogs. We believe this is a great development for the County of Surry, as it will bring a positive light to the county and go a long way toward restoring the damage done by what happened at Bad Newz Kennels.

In our work for chained dogs, we have an immediate and ongoing need for employees to work with our dogs and facility. We have purchased a commercial kennel license, and we have two staff members on site working for these dogs at all times. We have three areas fenced already behind the house for their safety and the safety of the neighborhood, and we have plans to fence the entire property so they may run without harming themselves or others.

We bought this facility to build a kennel where our rescued dogs can be rehabilitated and adopted out to new, loving homes and families. It is our understanding that commercial kennels are currently a by right use in the county, and as such we are also entitled to employees and an office to care for the dogs and the facility.

The majority of the traffic to the facility will be coming to visit our adoptive dogs and see how we are transforming the place.

We have been told we must request an exception for a small store space in the front of the house, contained within the office area measuring 12' x 12', which will sell books by Dogs Deserve Better and others on dogs and the property, as well as small items such as t-shirts, car magnets, bumper stickers, and pens. This is an incidental use only, as people visiting the kennel may purchase items if they wish to support our facility and our work.

We have plenty of parking off to the side of the house, and plan for a total of 20 people stopping by per week. Our open hours will be 9 a.m. to 5 p.m. daily.

We hope to build a positive community image both for our facility and for Surry County. If you all would like to stop by, we will be happy to show you around so you can see how well we are maintaining the grounds and the facility.

We would be denied a right to a "storefront", and approval for the office component was withheld until the next month to ascertain if we could "behave ourselves" with regards to the neighbors.

Us behave ourselves? Unbelievable.

I was already sick of the bullying, so I decided to stand up to them. It's not like our relationship could get much worse at that point, so at the next meeting I presented a much stronger statement:

DEAR SURRY COUNTY ZONING BOARD:

I read the recommendation to deny our application with disbelief. This recommendation is based on "concerns related to operation of the kennel as conveyed by adjacent property owners and confirmed by the applicant." Yet, were we not told repeatedly at the last meeting that the concerns brought up had nothing to do with the application?

And that's why the extra meeting was scheduled to educate us all on trespassing and animal control laws, during which no one mentioned any further beefs?

What concerns would these be that we confirmed? That one of our dogs got loose and went onto Mr. Hardy's property? Yet Mr. Hardy himself has two dogs that run up and down the road virtually every day in violation of a leash law, and often came onto our property before we got the left side fenced. We never complained about it, because we didn't feel it was the right thing to do.

I, in turn, never got angry at Mr. Hardy about it. In fact, I would have preferred to see him come charging up after his dogs rather than let them roam the neighborhood and potentially get hit by a car. I would welcome him to come onto our property any time he needs to get his dogs.

Everyone's dogs get out on occasion. Even Ms. Mack [Surry County Planning Community Develop Director] talked about a time her dog ran loose, and she was most concerned about quickly getting her dog to safety. Life is not cut and dry, and doesn't always go by the book. You have to have kindness, do your best, and take care of each other; not try to destroy people you don't even know and never even met.

We came to Surry County with the best intentions for our dogs, for the property, and for the county. I grew up on a 108-acre farm in Pennsylvania, and have always lived in the country whenever possible, so I know what country living is like. Since I bought my home in Pennsylvania 15 years ago, I never had any problems with my neighbors.

So what is the real issue here in Surry County, I would ask? One local person, speaking to the New York Daily News "on condition of anonymity" stated, "There is an unmistakable racial underbelly to the matter, with a white woman charging into town on the proverbial white horse to clean up the criminal misdeeds of young black men, among them an iconic figure in this part of Virginia."

I couldn't agree more that there appears to be an unmistakable racial underbelly to the matter, but it's not coming from me. Growing up in Pennsylvania, I was never taught to have racial prejudices, but coming here I can see that racial prejudice is alive and well. In this instance, it seems to be directed toward the white woman who dared to hope to build a rehab center for dogs on a property that created a bad name for Surry County.

I naively believed we'd be welcomed by Surry County so that the misdeeds of those gone before could be turned around and thereby give Surry County a better reputation.

But the way I was treated here last month was reprehensible.

When members of your board—along with Ms. Mack—came by our property for a tour unannounced, I welcomed them and did my best to answer all of their questions. Ms. Mack even commented that it was "too quiet" in the house.

Isn't that what Surry County wants?

Everyone was able to see that everything was exactly as I had stated and that all our dogs were well loved and well cared for.

That our center was clean, and that it is cleaned daily.

That we have already built three fenced areas and have made considerable progress toward fencing in the entire property, all on a shoestring budget and with mostly volunteer help.

Your comment to "permit the nonprofit entity an opportunity to demonstrate that the uses permitted by right can be responsibly managed" is as though you're speaking to a four year old, or about a four year old. I am 47 years old, and both my assistant and myself regularly work 14-hour days caring for our dogs and the property.

I served our country as a member of the United States Air Force, and my husband is retired Air Force. In my duties to my country, I served with men and women of all colors, backgrounds, and sexual orientation. To imply that either my staff or I came here out of racial prejudice is ludicrous.

Yet I am certain that we are experiencing racial and gender prejudice against us as being both white and women. The "anonymous quote" I read previously and the flimsy excuse for a recommended denial prove it in my mind.

Furthermore, you recommend to deny us our right to have an office with our kennel, but how can a by-right commercial kennel NOT be entitled to an office as part of that kennel? If our kennel were a breeding kennel, would there not be an office where the kennel bookwork was done, where people wanting to buy dogs came in and were serviced by staff, where deals were made? If our kennel were a boarding kennel, would there not be an office and staff who greeted the customers, where bookwork was done, and where payment for those services was made?

You mention that as a home-based business, we cannot have visitors on our site for fundraising purposes, yet you cannot deny us our right to conduct the business of our kennel. And the business of our kennel is a nonprofit, and as such we are continually fundraising for our center. You no more have the right to control our day to day activity than you can control that Mr. Hardy has friends over to his house for a barbeque and picnic.

This is America last time I checked, and just as the neighbors have a right to their lives—and we have tried very hard not to interfere with their lives—we have a right to our by right kennel license and the office and activities that go along with that kennel.

I would ask you today to stop the prejudice against us because of the color of our skin, our gender, and the fact that you wish it had ended better with Michael Vick. It didn't, and that ending affects Surry County's reputation as well.

We deserve to be treated fairly and equitably, and we seem to be doing 100% better than the last tenants of the 1915 Moonlight Road house. I believe that we have endeavored to give you all decent treatment, and we deserve the same in return.

We never would get Surry County's "permission" to sell items from our office. Instead, we told visitors what a "donation" could get them: for instance, if you donate $20 you can get a free t-shirt or two books.

They would also "allow" us to have two staff members living onsite, plus one additional person was "allowed" to come to work there. In the end, we said "ok, whatever you say" and ignored them, going about our business in the way that best suited our needs.

I was prepared to fight legally if forced into that position, but for the time being I would sit back, hoping they would wander off and torment some other well-meaning citizen.

Still today, I shake my head in disbelief about the way our organization and myself were treated by the leadership of Surry County, in comparison to Michael Vick. Do you think Vick was brought in front of the council and berated for chaining and breeding dogs on the property? For his peeps doing and selling drugs there? For holding fights in the sheds, with LOTS of guests and participants; for the dogs that were slain at the drop of a hat and whose bones litter the property?

No. No, I don't think he was.

On a further note of irony, and to put the utter foolishness of what went down in those zoning meetings into perspective, Surry County is home to a nuclear power plant, containing two reactors. In fact, much of the county, including 1915 Moonlight Road, is within the ten mile "don't even bother running, you're dead" zone should anything go awry. The plant has 900 employees.

There was a close call shortly before we bought the place in 2011, too. Wikipedia tells us:

• On April 16, 2011, a tornado touched down in the plant's electrical switching station, disabling primary power to the plant's cooling pumps and causing the backup diesel generators to activate without incident.

(That might have been when the tree went through our shed roof.)

I can't help but wonder what the zoning waivers looked like for those two nuclear reactors . . . hey, but don't you dare sell any t-shirts, Dogs Deserve Better!

The dreaded "storefront." Oh No!

The dogfighting sheds in late 2013. Photo by Rita Thomas.

CHAPTER NINE:

The Dogfighting Sheds

"THESE ARE IMPORTANT SITES THAT TELL US A LOT ABOUT WHAT IT IS TO BE HUMAN . . . FOR US TO REFLECT ON AND TRY TO BETTER UNDERSTAND THE EVIL THAT WE'RE CAPABLE OF."[3]—J. JOHN LENNON, PROFESSOR OF TOURISM AT GLASGOW CALEDONIAN UNIVERSITY, SCOTLAND

The most morbidly fascinating aspect of the property was the collection of sheds used in the dogfighting operation. Almost everyone who came to visit asked to look at them, although there were a few folks who said they didn't think they could handle it. Dog lovers felt a need to see where the crimes were committed, to understand the depths of the depravity involved in dogfighting. Most left deeply affected, and with a strengthened resolve to put an end to this horrific abuse of our "best friends".

The fight sheds the first day I looked at the property.

There were four sheds, two to the left and two to the right, all painted black. The buildings appeared hastily and poorly erected, especially compared to the pristine white house decorously situated at the front of the property. Three of the four sheds had spray-painted black interiors, too—even down to the windows—to keep anyone from seeing inside.

The only one not painted black inside was used as a med station, to patch up any dogs they actually wanted to keep alive after the fight. Two of the sheds still had syringes lying on the window sills when we moved in.

The first shed to the left (when facing them from the house) was used for training and housing dogs who were being readied for the fight. All that remained by the time we got there were kennel spaces, complete with 4-year old feces, cement dog bowls, and dog boxes. In the middle of the building stood a greased pole, which acted as the axle for a carpet mill long ago taken for evidence. Above the pole was a board with tether clips mounted in place, containing the initials BNK (Bad Newz Kennels) hand drawn in yellow.

"BNK" hand drawn on board where the carpet mill stood. Note the black window.

The far right shed consisted of darkened kennels for the injured and mothers with pups. This shed gave off a pervasively eerie feeling, the walls scraped with claw marks by dogs desperate to escape.

Dark and dreary shed with claw marks on the walls. Photo by Rita Thomas.

Finally, there was the two-story fight shed, closest to the house. When we first looked at the property in February, the white, stand alone bathtub the dogfighters used to wash dogs before a match remained on the ground floor of the shed. The dogs were bathed not for any luxurious reasons, of course, but to ensure no one was cheating by slipping poison onto their dog's coat. There was also a huge bin full of dog food—four year old, rotting dog food, that is.

Our agreement when putting the contract on the property was that everything that was left of the dogfighting ring needed to stay. Unfortunately, Todd Builders pulled a sneaky one, adding a codicil stating that he could remove anything belonging to him. As the property and everything in it belonged to him at the moment of sale, he absconded with the tub and food bin—for some unknown reason wanting his own momentos of Vick's dogfighting ring.

Not only had Ray Todd taken the tub and bin, but he dumped the old, rotten food on the ground outside the shed, leaving us to clean up the mess before our dogs ate it and became ill as a result.

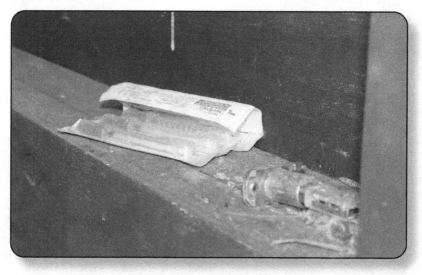

Syringes still lay on windowsills in two of the buildings.

There were still odds and ends left in the fighting shed, almost like it had frozen in time. Anything that the feds hadn't considered as evidence for their case against Vick and his buddies still remained as it was four years earlier. This included an ESPN mug, old collars, lots of rusty chains, some cement dog bowls, and, creepiest of all, a puppy calendar from 2007.

An old collar and an ESPN mug sit on a shelf in the fight shed. Photos by Rita Thomas.

A pull-down ladder leads to the actual fight arena. Dogs were carried or shoved up.

Jackets left in the fight arena, like they'd be right back for them. Photos by Rita Thomas.

Upstairs, where the dog fights actually occurred, was like stepping into a second time warp. There were two old sweat jackets tossed over camp chairs, an old stereo and speakers, cut out squares in the floor from where the feds tested the wood for blood, and old tan carpet remnants.

The windows were painted black, and dog scratches etched the walls.

If there is indeed a hell, I hope that this is one of the rooms dogfighters end up in, forced to fight for their lives day in and day out.

An old stereo still sits on the fight room floor. Photo by Rita Thomas.

Volunteers rip out carpeting and install rubber flooring for the dogs. Sloan is very helpful.

CHAPTER TEN:
Expert Advice, Interior Renovations, and Our First Adoption

"IT HAD BEEN A LONG DRIVE FROM EAST CENTRAL ILLINOIS TO THE GOOD NEWZ REHAB CENTER. BUT WHEN I ARRIVED I KNEW I WAS SUPPOSED TO BE THERE. TO DO WHAT I COULD, TO HELP MAKE RIGHT A WRONG."—REG GREEN, EARLY VOLUNTEER

*D*espite the harassment from county leadership and the neighbors, we were still tasked with moving forward with our dreams to turn the property into a first-rate facility for our clients. Our donors and the dogs were counting on us!

One of our early projects was the removal of carpeting in the family room and bottom floor master bedroom, as these were slated to be solely dog living areas. Kerry Krienetz, owner of a Central Bark Doggy Daycare franchise, flew down to advise us on how to make the place as dog-friendly as possible.

The finished flooring, much more dog friendly!

Based on her recommendations, we pulled up the carpet and replaced it with black rubber flooring of a type similar to their properties; we also installed crates in the second room with colorful blankets over them as doggie "bunks". Here dogs would eat and sleep safely at night and during naptime, unless they were too triggered by the close proximity to other dogs.

Kerry stressed the importance of a daily schedule for both the dogs and the staff, so we came up with the following, which we kept in place with minor revisions throughout my tenure.

Daily Schedule for Dogs at the Good Newz Rehab Center

This schedule is approximate, times may vary depending on other factors, but this gives you a general guideline for the day.

8:00 a.m. Daily schedule starts. Let dogs out for potty time. Dogs in large group get out first, then the dogs in smaller groups break out.

8:10 a.m. First walk. Walk dogs in big group first, let smaller groups stay outside in fenced areas unless weather is inclement.

8:40 a.m. Big group returns from walk. Switch and confine these dogs as needed for safety.

9:15 a.m. Last walk finished, last dogs walked remain outside with caretaker. Scoop poop and fill and clean doggie pools.

10:00 a.m. Feed dogs. Feed smaller groups together first. All dogs eat in crates for their safety and protection. When smaller groups are done, they go outside into separate areas for play time.

10:15 a.m. Feed large group of dogs, in crates unless exceptions are noted and known. Clean all dog bowls.

10:30 a.m. Begin daily cleaning chores. Both rooms, large room and smaller dog room, must be cleaned and mopped daily. Check and shake out all dog bedding and blankets. Anything dirty put into laundry room and begin day's laundry.

12:30 p.m. Chores should be done, this is training or play time with the dogs. Try to give all dogs attention.

2:00 p.m. Naptime. Crate dogs who sleep in crates, others nap in big room. This is caretaker 2-hour break time. Caretaker may nap in employee room upstairs, eat, or do whatever desired.

4:00 p.m. Second walk. Repeat above procedures for walking dogs.

5:00 p.m. Feed dogs second meal and clean bowls, same procedure as morning.

6:00 p.m.-9:30 p.m. Work on laundry, make sure all dogs get attention and clicker training.

9:25 p.m. Walk outside with dogs in big group and make sure everyone pees before bed.

9:30 p.m. Lights out. Dogs sleep in crates for safety, unless exceptions are noted. Caretaker off duty, can go home or overnight as scheduled.

We kept caretaker logs for each dog, and notes for medication and other special needs. We put these systems in place during our initial training with Kerry—even though we started with only six foster dogs—so that the kinks would be worked out by the time we upped our dog list to a max of 11-14 (until we could build our addition).

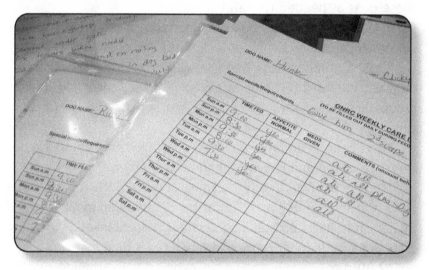

Sample dog logs.

Kerry also explained some of the struggles we'd undergo with fencing and separating dogs who didn't get along. Her help and advice were incredibly valuable in moving us in a positive direction, and God knows we needed some of that. Even though I'd been fostering dogs from my home for years, I'd never thought about nailing down a daily schedule and sticking to it so that the dogs grew to have a sense of security in the routine. It made a lot of sense.

Shortly after our arrival, we had our first adoption for one of the dogs who'd made the move with me: Hunter was going home!

Hunter had a pretty crappy life when I met him. He was tethered to a cement porch in central Pennsylvania, surrounded by trash, and hunched over in submission. Odds are good he was being struck on a regular basis, because he cowered and tried to get low to the ground, as if to say, "Please don't hurt me, I'll be good."

It was heartbreaking. I knew I had to get him out of there

posthaste, so I said "Yes, I'll take him with me right now," and had his caretaker sign him over to DDB; I drove him home, cleaned him up, and he was on to a better life.

Hunter before his rescue.

Hunter chews on a toy at the center.

For a big mastiff, he'd sure played it small.[*]

No worries, though, because Hunter didn't stay small for long! Soon he was full of himself, running and playing with the other fosters, and starting to own his size and mastiff demeanor.

---

[*] Watch video of his rescue at https://bit.ly/2MjTmCU

In Virginia, Hunter found a new "leash" on life, finally getting the family of his dreams.

Hunter swims for the first time.

Hunter's mom Jessica wrote:

"Hunter is getting along great in his new castle—and I say castle because he is king around here. He has met all of my family including dad, brother, mom, niece, etc. He follows me around every move I make, and sleeps right beside us on his big bed upstairs. I can't thank you enough for saving this dog—he is sooooooo special to Ellie and I."

The neighbor really liked his "No Trespassing" signs.

CHAPTER ELEVEN:

The Neighbor Gets Egg on His Face

*E*ven though Joe and I had just gotten married June 20th, we wouldn't be living together for at least another year. He had his career, and I had mine, and it seemed never the twain shall meet. Joe's work was in the DC area, and he'd accepted a four-month deployment to Afghanistan, plus he had a couple months training beforehand in Vegas.

I would be living onsite at the center in Surry County, Virginia, until I got it off the ground and the organization was financially solvent enough to hire a facility manager I could trust. Luckily for me, my house in Pennsylvania sold quickly, so I donated $1000 of the proceeds to the organization, and started paying DDB $400 a month rent for my room at the center, plus a portion of the utilities, too.

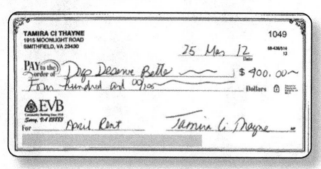

To my knowledge, I'm the only person who's ever paid to live there; since there were naysayers claiming I was just "living it up in the mansion"—on the organization's dime—I wanted to avoid any semblance of profiteering from the work of the nonprofit.

Truth is, I hated living onsite. As an introvert, the constant presence of other staff and visitors wore me down, and I had nowhere to go to recharge my battery and be free of the job. In fact, because we'd made the upstairs recreation room into a living room, my office had nowhere to go but in my bedroom. I was stuck just a few yards from my work 24/7, even in my "downtime" and at bedtime. It was a pretty miserable experience.

Even worse, if I actually WAS the only human onsite, that meant I was the sole caretaker for the dogs, and so I had to take on the daily schedule and ensure all their needs were met and the facility and dog yards were clean and neat.

We continued to have trouble with the neighbor to our left, Richard Clark, who was a white guy, I'm guessing in his mid 30's at the time. He was married with two young children, a little girl and a baby, and he continued to keep his many "No Trespassing" signs in place—even after we fenced directly in front of them—just to ensure we knew he still didn't want us there.

Message received.

Richard's petition hadn't gotten him too far, since they couldn't take away our right to a kennel license, although I'm sure they would have loved to do so. So what had been the point of it all? Why torture your new neighbors before they've even done anything to piss you off? It made no sense to me.

I couldn't help but wonder if he felt guilty about the beagles he kept penned on his property, and the next door presence of a group that stood against the practice needled him. The dogs lived in two lines of crowded kennels not far from our property line, and numbered in the neighborhood of 12-15 dogs. These dogs cried each morning and afternoon, pitifully, when we walked our dogs in the field, and the stench of their feces in the summer heat never failed to remind us of their suffering.

I also think he felt empowered to bully us because we were two women living alone there. I can't imagine the guy had the guts to beat on Vick's buddies like that, not if he wanted to live another day. But two women? Easy pickin's for the male bullies of this world.

One day he was riding his 4-wheeler with his daughter close to our property line, and a male volunteer—who I'd never met before—started yelling at him in front of the little girl. Richard took his little girl home, then came over to confront the man, and there ensued a screaming match between the two in our garage. I was mortified, and told the group that sent the volunteer out that he wasn't allowed to come back.

Even though Richard had treated us poorly since we'd arrived, I felt we had an obligation not to throw fuel on the fire. If they wanted to be cruel, we would stand up to them, but it wasn't good for our organization to sink to their level.

The next day I went over to their home to apologize and spoke to his wife, Kathleen. She seemed nice, and I felt like maybe we'd made some headway in neighborly relations as a result.

But the treatment didn't improve, and eventually Joe had had enough. We'd both felt unsafe in the house since DDB had moved in—the racial tensions, county harrassment, and overwhelming rage on both sides of the Vick debate making us feel like sitting ducks.

Todd Builders had fixed the bullet hole in the front window soon after the property sale, but I always wondered why and how it got there; it made me feel uneasy.

I wasn't a gun advocate, and Joe knew it. I didn't want the responsibility of a weapon on site, so we compromised and he bought me a stun gun for my safety. It did make me feel just a tiny bit better, although what are the odds I'd find it or even have it charged up when or if needed? Would I have been able to use it effectively if anyone attacked me? Doubtful. I'd probably be readily disarmed and shot in the head.

But it was something.

The next time Joe came to visit, before he left for Vegas, he'd decided to confront Richard himself, have a man-to-man talk with him. Open-carrying his pistol in his shoulder holster, Joe walked to the property line close to the beagles, hoping their barking would alert Richard to his presence. It worked. Soon Richard walked out, eyeing Joe warily.

Joe jumped right in. "I don't know why you think it's ok to treat my wife and her employee this way. They're just here trying to help dogs, working to right a wrong that occurred on this very property. What makes you think it's ok to bully them and push them around? You don't even know them."

"I'm just trying to protect my family," Richard replied, defensively.

"From what? Being licked to death by dogs? And you didn't have to protect your family from Vick and his cohorts? That was what I'd call a dangerous situation for your family! This is ridiculous," Joe fumed. "My wife doesn't deserve this kind of treatment, and I want it to stop."

Richard eyed Joe's gun nervously. "I thought you were planning to shoot me."

"No, but I want you to know my wife has someone backing her up, and I will defend myself if necessary. You've done nothing to earn my trust, that's for sure."

Richard thawed a bit after their discussion, and he told Joe he'd show me where Vick had kept the dogs chained. As it turned out, many were chained to car axles that they'd buried in the ground; as the dogs ran the perimeter, the axle would spin and the chain would remain untangled. This wasn't done for the benefit of the dogs, obviously, but to both lessen the workload for Vick's minions and build more muscle on the dogs as they ran the circumference reached by their chains.

Car axles that Vick's dogs lived chained to, removed from the field. Photo Rita Thomas.

We were able to find and dig up a few of the axles, but I'm sure a metal detector could find more still out in those fields today.

Not long after this final confrontation with Richard, Joe and I were eating breakfast together in Smithfield at the Main Street Restaurant; I noticed Richard's wife and kids eating at a nearby table with an older couple.

I nudged Joe, hunkering down in my seat. "Oh, crap, honey, there's the neighbor's wife, Kathleen!"

He can be a bit of a bumbler at times, so he said loudly, "Where?" and looked around conspicuously.

"Stop, they'll see you! Quit being so obvious," I whispered.

When he finally spotted the family, he got a weird look on his face. "I know that couple with her. I was stationed with them in England! Oh, my God, I think Kathleen's their daughter! I knew her when she was a teenager."

It was then that Kathleen noticed Joe, too, and her eyes widened. She promptly got up and approached our table. "Joe, is that you?"

Before I knew it, her father had joined us and introductions were made. Joe got caught up with Kathleen and her parents on where life had taken them since they'd been stationed together in England, while I sat quietly, half mortified and half amused.

Boy, did Richard look even more like a schmuck now! He'd treated a friend of his wife's family badly, not to mention said friend's wife.

He'd put my normally mild-mannered husband in the position of having to behave in a way I'd never seen before or since, and embarrassed his family by doing so.

I would have loved to be a fly on the wall at his home later when his wife and her parents told him they were long-time service buddies with my husband.

Richard never bothered us again after that day.

While we struggled, the dogs lived it up at the Good Newz Rehab Center.

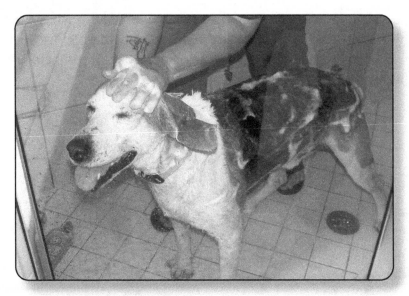

I give George his first ever bath.

CHAPTER TWELVE:

Speaking of "Huntin" Dogs

Our first new rescue after hitting the center was George, a hound from Sussex County, Virginia. George had a set of unusual appendages, in the form of two front nipples that dangled—and I'm talking four to six inches of swing, like he'd been overbred for years.

But he was most definitely a male. It was very confusing!

It was explained to us that when dogs are used for hunting purposes, their nipples can get caught on briars as they run the fields, create a drag on the delicate tissue that over time creates this kind of "situation." I was both mesmerized and horrified.

Volunteer Tamarah Brown, who would eventually end up

adopting George, said this about him. "George has scars all over his body. I try not to look at them when I bathe him for fear I will be overcome with sadness and won't be able to help with his healing."

Poor George, he had him some dangly bits.

"When he came to Good Newz he also had a unique issue that I've never seen before. Some say it was his nipples, I say it was loose skin because I'm in denial; whatever they were, they were visual reminders of neglect and abuse like the scars on the rest of his body. I loved George immediately but I had trouble with those pieces of skin. . . . One day I was playing with George and cuddling with him on the floor when one of the flaps hit me smack in the face. I thought I was about to die, but I didn't want George to think I was reacting to him in a negative way so I kept my feelings to myself."

We got George nipple reduction surgery. It seemed the right thing to do.

George had a gift, one I hadn't seen before or since, of letting himself out of the crate without destroying the locking mechanism. I finally set up a camera to figure out how he was doing it, and I would have sworn the dog was Houdini himself, he was out of that cage so fast!

Soon he was never crated again. My joke was that George couldn't be happier with the progress he'd made in training his humans!

George shows off his more manly chest.

George would be with us for eight months, as old hounds are certainly not "in demand" as adoptables, but he was finally taken home by Tamara for his own version of happily ever after.

You can watch video of George's trip to the good life here: http://youtu.be/blvRJAfjShY.

Cowboy and Anthony playing together in the yard.

CHAPTER THIRTEEN:
Elaine Goes Downhill

I liked Elaine, and thought I knew her, at least as well as you can know someone in a working environment. In Pennsylvania, she'd proven to be a very good employee, working hard and coming in with a proficient understanding of bookkeeping and how to do the office manager job.

Moving to the wilds of Surry County, Virginia, though, proved to be a lot more than either of us had bargained for. Not only did we feel unsafe in Vick's house given the attitude of those in the county toward us, but we were working long hours trying to get the place off the ground, were fielding constant requests to take in dogs we had no room for, were worried about money, and were under cyber-attack by a doctor in Washington state.

We felt like we were in a pressure cooker, and odds were good something would be blowing soon.

Turns out that something was Elaine.

Elaine was a single parent, and her adopted 15-year-old daughter Kali had moved to Virginia with us. She also soon asked us to house a teenage boy, Anthony, who had a very bad homelife in Pennsylvania, his mom having no problem sending him away to live somewhere else.

Kali was a disturbed teen with behavioral issues, and was often in trouble at school back in Altoona. In fact, she'd been sent to a special school for the learning and behaviorally challenged, where she was told it was her last chance. If she was thrown out of there, she had nowhere else to go. Surry was to be a fresh start for her, but I was admittedly nervous about cohabitating with an angry teenager.

Anthony was a tall, skinny kid, who just wanted to please everyone. He looked and acted like a beaten puppy, and he was especially drawn to any menfolk when they were around, volunteering to help with fencing or anything else they were working on.

Anthony's plight touched both Joe's heart and mine, and Joe said Anthony reminded him of one of his sons. We tried our best to be kind to the teens, and even named our first local rescue that November after the boy who touched our hearts, because the hound was sweet, beaten down, and skinny too.

Elaine and I bumbled through July, August, and September together, doing our best to get the place up and running and handle the myriad tasks of the organization as well as the center.

We took turns taking time off, she often going back to Pennsylvania to see her family, and me going to see my daughter and mother, as well as taking care of my house sale while Joe was training in Vegas.

Elaine told me when she started working for DDB that she wasn't much of a drinker, but we shared wine on occasion in the evening and talked about the events of the day, discussing our lives with one another.

I even bought her a case of those flavored alcoholic beverages at one point, as a way of saying thank you for all she'd done for the organization and the dogs since we'd come to the center.

Soon, Elaine became more and more stressed with the workload and attacks on DDB by locals and the doctor's sycophants, so we sent her to Joe's apartment in Northern Virginia for some R&R, making sure she had some wine and other self-pampering aids like bubble bath available, too.

Before long, it would come to light that Elaine was actually an alcoholic, and had failed to mention that important fact to me. She'd been kidding herself that she could handle a little here and there, and before she knew it, she was in deep trouble. It goes without saying that I'd have never bought her wine or other alcohol-containing beverages If I'd known . . . lordy, lordy.

Elaine had also represented the organization in Los Angeles that fall, where we were a finalist for the Stay Classy Awards, right at the time her drinking was hitting full stride. We dodged a bullet in that she didn't go MIA in a drunken stupor, or do anything major while there to affect our "classy" status. Well, at least not that I heard about.

It was safe to say that Elaine and I both struggled with poor self-esteem, and I know it's part of the human condition, especially for women. Even if in your heart you know you're doing something good, something right, when you're pummeled by the community you're trying to build in, beat up by people you don't even know online, AND still working many hours of overtime for a smallish salary, you might eventually have taken a fall too.

I don't really blame her for the meltdown. What I do blame her for is not telling me she was an alcoholic and needed to stay away from the sauce. That I could have easily understood, and made sure not to keep any in the house. I had enough experience with that after raising a teenage son . . . rather than be as naïve as my mother was while we stole her booze out from under her nose, I soon learned not to keep any around for Rayne to steal.

In early September, California area rep Deana Whitfield and

her partner, son, and mother moved over for her to work at the center. Deana was to be in charge of the dogs, while Elaine and I, for the most part, would go back to our intended work for the organization. Elaine would oversee all the front office work for the nonprofit and the center, while I would run activist campaigns and go on rescue missions for dogs in need.

All seemed to go well for the first week, with a lot of laughter and stories being told as we worked alongside one another. One day, though, I remember the three of us standing and talking together in the kitchen. For some odd reason, Deana asked, "So, if you all were in an abusive relationship, would you be the abuser or the abusee?"

"Abusee, definitely," both Elaine and I agreed.

But Deana said she'd be the abuser.

I immediately got a chill up and down my spine, and warning bells went off in my head.

As I would later find out, I was right to be alarmed.

In a memorable aside to the Elaine and Deana saga, both ladies claimed to be vegetarian. I had no reason to doubt it—I'd been one for nine years myself—so why would I question their word?

Yet one day, Elaine told me that Deana loved hotdogs and ate them all the time. Another day, Deana told me that Elaine was just pretending to be a vegetarian to get in my good graces.

What the hell, I wondered. *Who lies about something like that?*

My ex-husband, Bryn's father, knew me as a big meat-eater when we were together. But once I formed Dogs Deserve Better, I didn't feel it was right for me to advocate for one animal and eat another. So I soon turned to vegetarianism, and had never fallen off the wagon, deliberately at least; I do remember a couple of times when people told me something was vegetarian and it wasn't.

The ex used to ask my kids if I was eating meat yet, and when they'd say "No," he'd reply, "I'm sure she is, she's just hiding it from you."

But who wants to live their life like that?

I was disturbed by the apparent duplicity of both Deana and Elaine, but I shrugged it off, thinking it was their issue to deal with.

Sloan, sleeping peacefully. Keeping those young pups in line is a tough job!

A group of fencing volunteers takes a break to walk the dogs.

CHAPTER FOURTEEN:

Elaine is Shoved Over the Edge

*M*eanwhile, the doctor in Washington state (and, in hindsight, probably Deana too) was hard at work undermining what little was left of Elaine's self-esteem.

The doctor sent Elaine a big long message telling her she pitied her that she had to work for an ogre such as myself, and asked her to "come to the light. We have cookies."

Instead of discussing her worsening mental condition with me, Elaine kept it to herself, like her drinking. The first week of October, she drove home for a couple days to be with her family. She was scheduled to be back that Thursday, as I had a plane ticket and hotel reservations for an annual get together of my Air Force friends in Texas. I was so looking forward to it . . . you could never imagine how much! I couldn't wait to get out of there and laugh, reminisce, party, and relax with folks who'd meant so much to me in my early years. To be FREE.

But I would be disappointed.

Elaine went to Pennsylvania and slipped into a full-blown drinking binge. She never told me what was going on, though, and as Thursday rolled on by, I got more and more nervous that she hadn't come back yet. Text messages to her went ignored, or random messages about traffic problems came back.

At one point, she claimed she was on Rte. 10, close to the center, but there was "bumper to bumper traffic." Now, if you drove Rt. 10 between Hopewell and Smithfield, Virginia, at all, you would understand just how laughable that comment was. We're talking a two-lane road with minimal traffic at all times. It would indeed later become a joke for Joe and I anytime we were late or goofing around when we were supposed to be somewhere.

"Sorry, honey, bumper to bumper traffic."

Without Elaine's return, my trip was cancelled, as there was no one to care for the dogs. Their needs came before all else—naturally—so there was no question of staying or going. I stayed.

I missed my plane, lost my money for the ticket, and missed the reunion; needless to say I was not a happy camper.

Deana was still living locally, but she had quit as dog care manager after only two weeks, saying she was too afraid that the dogs would fight. She'd had a foster dog die as a result of a fight in her home in California, and couldn't get past her fear. Why would you take a job as a dog care manager if you couldn't handle being around the dogs? It made no sense.

I understood the fear, and could have respected it, as I too had residual fear of dog aggression. I'd been attacked by a foster dog, a chow chow, at my home in Pennsylvania in 2008—sending me to the hospital in an ambulance—and it had left me with my own issues surrounding dogs that I didn't yet know or trust.

But the thing was, Deana had flown to Smithfield to visit the area and let me know if she wanted the job before moving her family east. I'd held the position for her—because I'd promised—

and was irritated that she'd quit after such a short time.

I was SOL.

Elaine showed up in the middle of the night Friday night.

I didn't trust myself to talk to her, as I'd lost my vacation, my escape, and my money because of her actions. I didn't want to scream and yell at her, so I had to stuff it all down inside. The next morning I still couldn't look at her. "I expect you to take care of these dogs the rest of the weekend, because I'm getting out of here. Got it?" I bit out. She looked the worse for wear, but nodded sheepishly and went to walk the dogs.

I packed a bag and drove to Norfolk, where I found a hotel with a pool I could sit beside to lick my wounds and try to find some inner peace. It was in short supply.

Deana texted that she and her partner Katie would go over and check on Elaine later in the day. "Don't knock yourself out," I grumbled to myself, just as angry at her as I was at Elaine.

Admittedly, the lingering anger and frustration was interfering with any plans for relaxation. After all, I was paying for yet another hotel, I needed to try to enjoy it!

That afternoon the text messages from Deana started:

"Elaine's drunk."

"The kids have been caring for the dogs. The place is a mess."

"Elaine's starting to yell and curse at everyone."

"Elaine's out of hand."

"Tamara Brown came to help. She's a recovering alcoholic too, so she thought maybe she could handle her."

"We had to call the police. Elaine won't settle down."

Elaine ended up hospitalized; it was either that or spend the night in jail for disorderly conduct.

I lost more money on yet another hotel, because I had to pack up and go home so I would be there for the dogs the next morning.

Elaine spent the next few days in the hospital, and I had to step up to care for Kali and Anthony as well, making them dinner and trying to help them get through a trying time without feeling like they were unwelcome at the center.

When she did come back, sober now, I sat her down and had a long talk with her. "I'm really sorry for everything you're going through, Elaine, but I can't have an employee that can't be trusted with the dogs and the organization while I travel for work or get my own shot at R&R. I have to let you go."

She understood, but said, "Look, I really don't want to move back to Altoona; I came to Virginia to make a new life for myself and Kali. Can I stay here for two more weeks while I look for another job and a place to live? I'll volunteer while I'm here, too, to pay for room and board. I'll help train another office manager, too," she added hopefully.

I acquiesced, even though I really didn't feel it would be good for me or the dogs. But I wasn't a monster—I knew now that she was sober Elaine felt badly enough about everything that had happened.

Unfortunately, I was right to be uncomfortable with allowing her to stay. Elaine was supposedly out looking for jobs a lot in the following days, and didn't help much around the center. She spent any remaining time in her room, and I would later learn she was up there drinking. The following Saturday she left with Kali and Anthony in her car, but instead of looking for jobs or a place to live, she bought wine and got drunk in her vehicle. She ended up getting a DUI and spending the night in jail, while Kali and Anthony were brought back to the center.

I made the three of us some faux chicken soup, and the two glumly ate while they told me the story. They were lucky she hadn't wrecked with them in the car! She'd just stopped along the road out in the countryside and downed a bottle of wine, then passed out behind the wheel. The kids couldn't even wake her up, which led me to wonder if there were drugs involved, too.

Well, this was certainly a fine mess.

I'd planned not to allow her back into the center when she got out of jail, but she somehow was released and found her way back in the middle of the night. When I woke up the next morning to discover she was there, I was beside myself. "This is it, Elaine, the end. Enough," I said. "Pack up and leave, today. You can arrange to get your stuff sometime in the next week or two, but you can't stay here anymore."

She refused to leave the premises, though, and for the second time in a week we were forced to call the police for help. When they balked at getting involved, I told them I didn't own the home . . . the house belonged to the nonprofit, and as she was no longer an employee, she was not allowed on the property.

The deputy dutifully corralled her and herded her toward his vehicle. On the way there she had a full Jerry Springer style meltdown, running back and trying to physically attack me, screaming and yelling, while the officer grabbed her by the arms and dragged her away.

When it was all over, I was shaking and upset, and went into the kitchen to collect myself. I grabbed my iced tea off the counter and took a long swallow, only to get a mouthful of bug spray instead.

Great. Now I'd been poisoned, on top of everything else.

```
VA0900000 Surry County Sheriff's Office

--------------------- CFS REPORT# 2011-003648 ---------------------
CALL TYPE: 100-30 OTHER/UNKNOWN PROBLEM      AGENCY: 4-SHERIFF
DISPATCHER: R217-Ray,Nancy G                 RECEIVED:10/22/2011 14:11
JURISDICTION: 181-Surry                      HOW RECEIVED: 6-Other
DISPOSITION: 01-Report Needed                ACTIVITY: 3-Investigate
------------------------- COMPLAINANTS ---------------------------
TYPE          NAME                           PHONE           PID
COMPLAINANT   THAYNE,TAMIRA C                                00514949
VICTIM        THAYNE,TAMIRA C                                00514949
SUSPECT       ,KALI                                          00514950
--------------------------- ADDRESSES ----------------------------
CALLER    001915    MOONLIGHT              RD
OCCURRED  001915    MOONLIGHT              RD
----------------------------- UNITS ------------------------------
UNIT   AGENCY  RECV   DISPATCH  ENROU ARRIV  TRANSPORT  CLRD  RETURN
                      ALRM1 ALRM2            ENROU ARRIV       STATION
10      SHERIFF 14:11                                   14:59
        Handled by Deputy
--------------------------- COMMENTS -----------------------------
Dispatcher:R217@10/22/2011 14:26:17
KALI                PUT SOME REPEL INSECT REPELLANT IN A DRINK BELONGING
TO TAMMY THAYNE AS SHE WAS EXITING 1915 MOONLIGHT AFTER BEING EVICTED. MS
CONFESSED TO U-10 BENNY BACK AT THE SURRY COUNTY SHERIFFS OFFICE.
```

The police report of what shall henceforth be known as "the bug spray incident."

I immediately called the deputy who'd just been there and told him either Elaine or Kali had poured bug spray in my drink.

When he asked Kali about it, she admitted to it right away.

"Ma'am, do you want us to charge her with attempted poisoning?"

I couldn't stop shaking and crying.

"Yes, yes I do." I was dumfounded; after I'd stepped up to care for Kali and Anthony while her mom was hospitalized and jailed for her drinking binges, this was the thanks I got.

> 01/02:Mk oh btw this is Kali. Haha how did ur mom like ur drink:)

> **Kali P**   Feb
> Hey brynnan I hope ur mom liked her drink. And u better watch what u say

The deputy never did charge Kali with a crime. I might have been ok with that once I calmed down—after all, she was a minor—except she then bullied my daughter back in Altoona, getting ahold of her cell phone number and texting her and taunting her about it, asking "how'd your mom like her drink?"

This was a person who obviously had no remorse and no conscience.

The next week Elaine's mother brought a U-Haul to pick up her things.

To my knowledge, Elaine never was apprehended and forced to come back for her DUI hearings. Once in awhile a Wight County Sheriff would come by the property looking for her, even though I'd informed them numerous times she'd moved back to the Altoona, Pennsylvania area.

I never heard from Elaine again. I spoke with an Altoona

police officer about Kali's actions in regards to my daughter, but once again, nothing was done about it.

With today's social media, bullying is rampant and the victims typically have no recourse, unless they're rich and have a team of lawyers to keep the perpetrators busy. Unfortunately, abusers usually pick the easy targets, and leave those who can defend themselves alone.

That day, while all the shameful histrionics were going down, we had a new volunteer onsite, Leslie Thibeault. I didn't know Leslie well, she'd only recently started coming out on the weekends to volunteer, but I was so embarrassed that she'd been a party to that horror show. Through it all, I clearly remember Leslie quietly going about her business, doing dog laundry, petting and brushing dogs, while the world melted down around us, and the trash TV vibe ruled the day.

It was like bringing a complete stranger home for dinner, and all the family crazy you wanted to keep smushed up under the rug came oozing out and splashed acid all over your guest's pant leg.

Leslie took it in stride, but I was mortified, sure this would be the next thing to get back to the doctor who'd been trying to destroy us.

Yet it never did, and to this day Leslie and I are still friends. Because once someone witnesses that level of insanity—and still comes back to volunteer—she's earned a spot in my heart for life.

I was also mortified that we'd had to call the county for help twice in a week. Given that they already wanted us gone, the last thing we needed was to give them more ammunition.

Leslie would turn out to be an ongoing and very dedicated volunteer for the first two years as we worked to bring our facility to fruition. In fact, Leslie and her partner in no-crime, Melanie Gilbert, would prove to not only be a volunteer support system for me, but an emotional one as well. They came faithfully most every Saturday or Sunday, to give back to the world and get some of that precious doggy lovin'. As soon as they arrived, they'd jumped right in to help, doing whatever was needed:

they cleaned, socialized, walked dogs, and even built fences.

It seemed there was always another van load of fencing supplies.

At a time in my life when I was as down as I'd ever been . . . when the hits seemed to come from all areas and all avenues, these two women helped me believe in the goodness of human nature. I could never forget their gift to me, and to our dogs, during that difficult time.

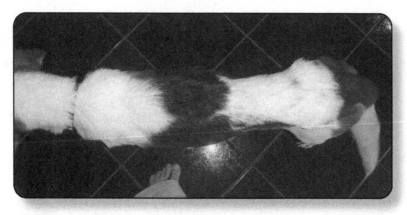

Photo of Anthony from above shows just how skeletal he was.

CHAPTER FIFTEEN:

Our First Local Rescue, Carried to the Center

O ne day in November Joe was at the property by himself while I ran out to the store, and a girl came walking down the road with a skinny hound draped around her shoulders.

She rang the gate buzzer, and he went out to meet her.

"Is there any way you can take this hound?" she asked. "He lives up the road in a pen at my uncle's house. He's a little slow, so all the other dogs get all the food, and he rarely gets any. He's losing more and more weight, and I'm worried about him. My uncle said you can have him."

Joe was taken aback by his plight and his obvious starvation, but he didn't want to respond for me. "The woman who runs the center is out at the store, but she'll probably be back within the hour. Can you come then to talk to her?"

She nodded her head and looked down, then picked the dog

up and carried him back to her uncle's house.

When I got home he described the dog to me, and I was so upset . . . luckily, we'd just had two spots open up at the center with adoptions, but even if we hadn't, I wouldn't have had the heart to turn away a dog in such obvious need.

It wasn't long before I spotted the teen walking down the road again, carrying the skeletal hound dog. She told me the same story she told Joe, and I was horrified to see how scrawny the poor dog was. Without hesitation I told her, "Yes, we'll take him," and had her sign him over to us.

We immediately fed him his first bowl of food, which he scarfed down, and then the first of three baths—the stench was unimaginable.

Joe and I named him Anthony, after the skinny boy Elaine had brought to the center. We would soon find out he was suffering from mild kidney damage, which the vet thought was probably from the medicine hunters give hounds to kill heartworms.

Anthony runs in the field during our first snowfall of the year. He'd become gorgeous.

We put him on a special kidney diet and he soon filled out, becoming one of my very favorites. Anthony carried a floppy, furry toy in his mouth at all times, and if anyone tried to take it from him he threw a royal fit. Anthony found a home of his very own in New Jersey, where he was well-loved for the remainder of his days.

Why would people try to take this home from the dogs? I couldn't get it.

CHAPTER SIXTEEN:
Outside Forces Continue to Hit Hard

Deana rode with me to pick up three dogs from one of our former area reps, Shannon Allen, while her girlfriend Katie worked the center as our new dog care manager.

Shannon had been the rep who suggested we buy the place, then—suddenly and without any legitimate explanation—flipped sides and joined the good Washington doctor in plotting our demise. I guess she liked cookies.

I'd never met Shannon Allen in person, she'd never been to our facility, nor had she visited the organization when I ran it out of my home. Yet she, bizarrely and cruelly, went to the media and told them that I was misusing organizational funds. Why?

I was blindsided, once again.

I've found that the media loves a bad news story, even when they have no evidence to support the allegations; this is incredibly irresponsible, given that as a nonprofit we depended on donors to stay afloat.

If the allegations were proven true, through some kind of actual EVIDENCE, then so be it. But there was no evidence, because the allegations were false. Shannon Allen had no access to our bookkeeping, and she provided them with nothing except a general allegation of misconduct.

That didn't stop the media from running news stories about it.

I called at least one reporter in and told her to take a look at our books. We opened our quickbooks, and asked her what she wanted to see. She, of course, had no idea where to even begin to look.

Joe sent the following email to that same reporter, Laurie Simmons:

> Reporting on all you had? Is that enough for WTKR? Did you do any research into these allegations or the person professing them before you reported on them, besides ringing a non-operational call button on the gate?
>
> Shannon has never met Tamira and has no connection to the finances of DDB. Are you aware that Shannon is a member of a Facebook Community whose sole purpose is to bring down Dogs Deserve Better? They are rejoicing on their page because you ran a story that casts a negative light on DDB. You did exactly what they wanted.
>
> You reported on the carport without confirming its purpose. The carport is to be used for outside shade for the dogs that elect to go outside, because there is no natural shade in that area adjacent to the home. The application to Surry County shows the proposed location, which is in a fenced area behind the house.
>
> This is something you would have found out if you had waited to run the story after you made more than

a cursory attempt to garner information. The last thing Tamira cares about is her van, which has been destroyed by dogs on the inside—she would never get a carport for it.

Tamira is a great person who has suffered the abuse of this FB community for five months now—and thanks to your news station, they are closer to their goal of destroying DDB. You can't throw around words like misappropriation of funds and stolen funds without proof. By reporting on them you are legitimizing their allegations. You and your station should be ashamed of the quality of your reporting.

Yet this didn't change the story or the fact that Shannon Allen also started making the very same allegations online, in different forums such as CNN's ireport.

We would later find out that what Shannon was accusing me of doing was exactly what she'd done from Virginia Tech: embezzle money.

Just before leaving the organization, Shannon posted this:

"I wouldn't affiliate myself with an organization that does the things that [Dr. Fiala] is claiming. I have a good relationship with Tami, that doesn't mean we don't disagree at times, but in the end I KNOW Tami is about and only about saving animals. If I for one moment I doubted that, I would quietly move on. I picked up a chained dog around 4:00 a.m. one morning after receiving a call. Vespa had been mauled while chained and escaped. I don't know how long she was on the run with her injuries but was she severely septic. I asked Tami if we should let her go or try to save her. Tami said, 'Save her!' Two days and $1500 later, Vespa died at the ER clinic. Tami was there for me at 2:00 a.m., two days before Christmas when Vespa died. I will always be grateful for that."

Apparently not THAT grateful, now, eh?

Here's an article we found about Shannon's embezzlement from Virginia Tech:

September 19, 2002
**EX-TECH WORKER PLEADS GUILTY
TO EMBEZZLEMENT CHARGES**
THE ROANOKE TIMES

A former Virginia Tech employee accused of misusing state credit cards handed over a $36,000 cashier's check Wednesday and earned a plea agreement that reduced four felony charges to misdemeanors.

Shannon E. Allen, 28, of Pembroke, pleaded guilty to the misdemeanor embezzlement charges in Montgomery County Circuit Court. Circuit Judge Ray Grubbs ordered her to serve two years on probation and suspended a 48-month jail sentence.

Allen was indicted in April for putting $36,451 in personal items on two university credit cards between April 8 and Dec. 2, 2001. She had been an employee of the department of near environments, in which students learn about interior design, housing management, apparel design, personal finances and other consumer resources.

Dogs Deserve Better obviously should have been doing background checks (or even basic googling might have been wise) before allowing reps to come onboard with our organization. As time went on, it became more and more apparent that just because someone loves—or claims to love—dogs, it doesn't make them an upstanding or particularly moral person. I now believe there are just as many criminals in the animal rescue world as there are in the rest of society.

Shannon then posted on groups all over the east coast claiming that DDB (and I) had abandoned our dogs with her. However, I'd been lecturing her for the past couple years on taking in too many dogs. I ended up creating the following post about the issue:

The Dogs Deserve Better Area Rep program is very unique, in that not only are we geographically scattered across the entire country—and sometimes even world—but each rep has in the past been given the utmost freedom of choice and control over his/her area.

This meant that first and foremost a rep was required to be an adult, to behave like an adult, and to make adult decisions as to her/his ability to rescue dogs, place dogs, and take physical responsibility for any dogs rescued in her/his area. In addition, reps made decisions about talking to people with chained dogs, running educational booths, building fences, and starting grass-roots efforts to change laws for man's best friend to prohibit chaining.

I never asked or told reps to go rescue a certain dog. I didn't feel that was my decision to make. Rescuing a dog is a big commitment, and I would make that commitment for myself and for myself alone. If I were able to take a certain dog into my home and foster him/her, I might ask a closer rep to facilitate rescuing the dog and getting him/her to me.

I typically fostered as many as six dogs at a time, out of my home, which also doubled as the organizational headquarters. There was not any kind of magic castle in which to put dogs who needed rescue. Either a rep took responsibility for them, I took responsibility for them, or we tried to network with other rescues for placement for the dogs.

Our reps who behaved as adults understood this from day one, and made sure when they decided to step down that all their fosters were adopted or in foster homes which they would continue to monitor until the dogs found permanent placement.

For example, former rep Penny Gummo elaborates: "When I was with Dogs Deserve Better, I was told I wouldn't get vetting paid without prior approval and I never assumed that any dog I rescued would be physically taken in by Dogs Deserve Better. I don't know why anyone else would think they could do anything they please without approval. Rescue WOULD be much easier if we could just give the dogs to someone else once we rescued them . . . "

In fact, Shannon Allen typed on April 2, 2011: "I feel responsible for every dog I adopt for the entire life of that dog. I assume at any given time an owner is going to call me and say they can no longer keep their dog. Maybe I am a control freak, but it is important to me to make sure that all dogs I adopt out are safe, happy, and healthy for the entire lives."

We had been having trouble with Shannon as a rep for awhile with behaviors that were indicative of hoarding, or at least an inability to judge how many dogs she could handle at any one time.

Even though I did not like to interfere in reps decision-making processes, I was compelled to start counseling her about rescuing too many dogs for one person to handle. On April 5, 2010, I wrote the following: "I'm a little concerned that you're getting in over your head with the number of dogs. How many do you have right now?"

On February 7, 2011, I wrote her the following: "As I told you before, you personally cannot save them all. You have 19 dogs at your house, and you are costing the org a fortune in boarding. IT HAS TO STOP."

Yet Miss Allen continued to ignore me and created vet bills in the organization's name at three different vets that we had no knowledge of. No reps were allowed to create accounts in the organization's name, period, and Ms. Allen knew this, but she continued anyway.

Melody Whitworth, area rep coordinator at that time, worked with Shannon and I to come to an agreement where DDB would immediately take three of her foster dogs into the center.

Hence the five hour road trip to western Virginia.

When Deana and I got to Shannon's home that day, there was something amok. The upstairs of the house looked clean enough, but there was a stench emanating from somewhere that assaulted the nostrils. It had to have been coming from the basement where she was keeping the dogs.

I reserved the right to choose which dogs I felt would fit in best at our center, but Shannon wouldn't allow us to go down into her basement to see her foster dogs. We stood outside while her husband went in and got one dog at a time, bringing him/her out to meet us.

Those who have nothing to hide, hide nothing. There's no place this is more true than in animal rescue, in my opinion. If Shannon didn't have something fishy going on in her basement, she would have readily let us see the place.

We decided on a dog named Abel, who we would later rename Cowboy, and two huskies, Rose and Storm. All three dogs had been rescued from chains, and we looked forward to giving them better lives.

I was humbled at the mistakes I'd obviously made in our area rep program. No one should have been allowed to represent our organization in another area of the country without first passing a home visit and background check—at a minimum. Shannon was not the first rep to cause us major heartache and disappointment, but she would be the last for me.

Even though we took three of the dogs that Shannon had rescued and committed to, the former area rep continued to badmouth us at every opportunity. She now complained that we took her three most adoptable dogs, and left her with only unadoptable ones.

Shannon reminded me of a toddler who, no matter how many hoops you jumped through trying to entertain them, continued to whine to get more attention.

A couple months later, I would end up meeting her half way for another dog, AND providing her with dog food for her remaining foster dogs. I would also include her in our Christmas campaign, gifting her seven remaining foster dogs with a $100 Petsmart gift card each, for a total of $700 in dog supplies.

Two years later, Shannon would offer a public apology of sorts, but it was way too little way too late in my opinion. She'd well proven all I needed to know about her by that time.

"Now that the tables have turned and I am on the receiving

end of what I had previously dished out, I feel that I have come full circle and am opening my eyes to the REAL agendas of the 'anti-rescue' hate groups. This brings me to a point that I feel I need to address my relationship with Dogs Deserve Better. In short, my relationship with DDB can best be defined as neutral. I have zero interest in tearing anyone down [anymore?] and I appreciate the fact that, despite the 'bad blood', they have reciprocated. What I can say with absolute certainty, is that if I could go back to 2011 when I resigned from DDB, I would have done things MUCH differently. And since I am laying it all out there; I DO owe an apology to Tamira Thayne. Rather than contacting her directly to discuss our differences, I took to the 'airways', cut her off, and blocked her from defending herself."

Just one of the vet bills Shannon Allen had made in our name without our permission.

When she asked me if that was a sufficient public apology, I told her:

"Quite honestly, no, it's not enough. You have perpetuated and claimed blatant lies and falsehoods about me for years. You act like WE were fighting, but in reality it was only you smearing me. I barely said two words about you on Facebook, I defended myself twice to my recollection.

"In fact, I have no idea what I ever did to you to suddenly make you flip. To my knowledge I never did anything to harm you before you turned on me. Which makes your betrayal the most bitter.

"So unless you can specifically admit that you lied about me being a felon AND that I NEVER misused organizational funds, it's not enough."

With the advent of the internet, it's alarming the amount of harm people like Shannon Allen and the Washington state doctor can do to an organization simply by relentlessly attacking them with lies.

We even, at one point, had someone who was riled up by the doctor ask to come and volunteer at our center so she could "punch me in the face."

> **Jessica Wiegratz** I'll take him!!I live in VA!!I'm in Dinwiddie....about 20 mins from the kennel property,I should go work there just to punch that stupid c**t in the face....oh yes,I DID call her a c**t!!

> Jessica Wiegratz
> Does the Good Newz Kennels need help!?I live in Dinwiddie...I know extra hands can be helpful!!Also...do they need any fosters??

I felt beaten and alone, and that there was no one I could trust.

I will never be able to put into the words the depths of the despair I felt during those dark days. Still today, I dream about that time, and when I wake I can remember the exact feeling of melancholy that's left behind. It's a nuance, as if each tiny difference in feeling were a key on a piano, but there's no name for the individual keys, only the octave called "sadness."

Little did I know, things were just getting started.

Cowboy on his chain, a miserable boy.

CHAPTER SEVENTEEN:
Abel, aka Cowboy

Cowboy was one of the three pups we brought over from Shannon Allen's house, and I quickly fell in love. He was so big and squishy, and was splotched in black and white—putting me more in mind of a cow than a dog—hence the name change to Cowboy.

It fit.

There were many evenings he'd lay on a kuranda bed in the smaller dog room, and I'd go in and snuggle with him, squeezing him gently and telling him I loved him. He was one of the hardest for me to let go.

Cowboy was slow moving, easy going, and soon became fast friends with Rose, Storm, and Lilly, too.

And me.

Cowboy loving every second of the Girl Scouts' attention.

I would later write this about him after taking this photo: "One day Cowboy was living a life of solitude and misery, and then suddenly there he was—surrounded by 15 girl scouts who were loving on him, cuddling him, doting on him. He ate up every second of those young angels' attention, taking it all in.

"I can't see this photo without getting a little teary-eyed, but it also brings me joy, opens my heart to the possibilities that exist for animals.

"Cowboy reminds me to write on their behalf. He reminds me that all dogs, all animals, deserve this kind of freedom and respect from humans.

"He reminds me."

Cowboy later got a home in Massachusetts, and his family came to chain out with me at the state Capitol, standing up for dogs who lived in the same conditions as he did. This kind of community connection highlights the reach that comes with raising our voices and sharing stories of those lucky enough to be saved.

One of two doggie doors we installed to the back deck, so dogs could go in and out as needed.

CHAPTER EIGHTEEN:

Deana Can Help

"IF YOU WANT TO DESTROY AN ORGANIZATION, ANY ORGANIZATION, YOU DESTROY IT FROM WITHIN, YOU DESTROY IT FROM WITHOUT AND THEN WHAT YOU DO IS YOU CONVINCE EVERYBODY THAT YOU'RE DOING THE RIGHT THING,"—U.S. GENERAL MCRAVEN, OCT., 2019[4]

When Deana and I were driving over to pick up dogs from Shannon Allen, she and I were discussing Elaine's fall, and the fact that I now needed to hire a new office manager.

As luck would have it, Deana had some experience in this area, and could slip right into the position!

At the time, of course, this would seem especially fortuitous to me . . . I wouldn't have to advertise for someone, interview anyone; Deana ostensibly knew and loved the organization, and could quickly and easily step right into Elaine's shoes. She also claimed she knew bookkeeping.

The fact that she'd only lasted two weeks in the dog manager role was pushed to the side, with the assumption that it was just a bad fit for her.

But office manager? That was a different story.

Her partner Katie had already started as dog caretaker, and with Deana stepping in as office manager, we were back up to three people.

Maybe I could actually get back to the work of managing the organization? I was thrilled.

It didn't take long for things to once again take a turn for the worse.

Katie was, ostensibly, so happy in her new career working with dogs that she quit her anti-anxiety medication. *Uh oh*, I thought. *This will not end well for me or DDB*. Working at the center in those early days was a reason to go ON medication, not OFF. I was on edge.

Sure enough, within weeks Katie was flying off the handle, yelling at the dogs, and reacting angrily to the point where volunteers started coming to me about it. Then she became furious that I brought in more dogs "without her approval", even though I hadn't been aware that was required.

Katie felt we should have a max of 11 dogs onsite, and—due to outside pressure to rescue even more dogs—I believed we needed to push it to 14. This would leave two packs of seven for playtime, but we could also rotate a couple of dogs upstairs with me and a couple could hang out with Deana in the front office. It was doable.

Katie quit in a huff.

Despite my repeated hopes that things would get better, things were not progressing well, at all.

To give credit where credit is due, Deana did one thing that was highly beneficial to Dogs Deserve Better during her time with us. I've now come to realize it was precisely because of her criminal mindset that she understood what was happening, because I was clueless. It turned out the county had given us a private or home-based kennel license instead of the commercial kennel license we needed and qualified for as a nonprofit. Deana figured it out and went up to the county offices, not letting up until we had the license we were entitled to.

Her action may have gone a long way toward getting the county management off our backs. Commercial kennels would be entitled to more staffing and less nitpicking over small and inconsequential items than a home-based one would.

By March of 2012, Deana was embezzling from the organization, but it would be months before I would find out.

Joe installs a second set of steps off the back deck for two entry and exit points.

Anthony and George soak up the attention from the Girl Scouts.

CHAPTER NINETEEN:

Thanksgiving with the Dogs

That first Thanksgiving I spent with the dogs, and I wrote this to our followers:

Tomorrow I will be on duty, spending Thanksgiving with the 14 dogs at the Good Newz Rehab Center in Smithfield, Virginia. At first I felt deprived that I wouldn't have the traditional Thanksgiving with my family in Pennsylvania, but then I realized that all 15 of us have more to be grateful for than I can even put into words.

These 14 dogs would very likely be dead or still chained or penned if it weren't for Dogs Deserve Better opening our doors and our hearts to them.

Without your belief in us, we would not have gotten our center off the ground, would not have made that crucial first step in the long road to building a mecca for formerly chained dogs.

Without your continued support, laws would not be changed, children would not be educated about the proper way to care for their best friend, and hope for suffering dogs would still be light years away.

Without the hard work of the volunteers and area reps who have rededicated themselves to working for chained dogs nationwide, even more dogs would be alone, forgotten, and suffering tomorrow.

I'd like to extend a big ol' Southern THANK YOU, from our table to yours: Tami, Sloan, Cowboy, Spotty, George, Jada, Shawnee, Riley, Ebby, Storm, Rose, Hef, Polly, Anthony—and our new girl who just arrived today from former rep Holly Lyttle in Oklahoma—Lilly.

We are grateful for you. Please have a blessed Thanksgiving, and know you've helped make so many dreams come true.

I never felt more thankful than watching our dogs run with joy and abandon in our field.

One of my favorite Cowboy photos.

CHAPTER TWENTY:

Online Defamation Campaign by Washington State Doctor

The first time I remember being bullied by a peer I was in seventh grade. I'd worn a dress to school that day, which I rarely did, and I was proud of looking my best. I felt good about myself. When I got off the bus at the transfer point, someone grabbed my books and said "You're gonna be in a fight." I was scared, there's no doubt about it. I wondered who I would be fighting and why.

Turns out it was the biggest, meanest girl in my class, Elyse Klemann. I had no idea why she was beating me up, and I had no one to help me. My brother and my friends stood by and watched, too scared to come to my defense. Her friends were the potheads and other bullies, and they took turns pushing me back into her, at which point she would grab me by the hair and swing me around. I gave her a scratch on her neck, something that showed some tiny scrap of courage, some kind of will to fight back.

I'm pretty sure if I were in the Hunger Games that day, I would have been the first one killed at the Cornucopia. I closed down after that, subconsciously believing that if you stand out in any way, you will be attacked.

It was many years before I felt willing to let my light shine again. In forming Dogs Deserve Better, I had to face the possibility of death at the hands of a dog chainer or someone else who didn't like what I stood for. I decided these dogs deserved that much dedication from me, and I commenced with my plan to stand up for their freedom despite the pain it brought on for myself.

I thought I'd gotten past my fear of bullies, but beginning the year DDB bought Vick's Bad Newz Kennels, we were subjected to an extensive campaign of abuse by a doctor from Washington state.

> RE-POST from Suzanne Fiala:
>
> NOTICE: We are HERE, and we pursue our newly stated goals tirelessly. FIRST on the list to expose and eradicate is DOGS DESERVE BETTER founded by Tamira Ci Thayne. I have been

Dr. Suzanne Fiala made it known her goal was to destroy Dogs Deserve Better, and hence me. But who was most harmed by her and those she convinced to do her bidding? The very dogs they purported to love.

Cheryl Dellasega, the psychologist who authored the book *Mean Girls Grown Up*, said women commonly attack other women, particularly in cyberspace.[5]

"I hear about adult women retaliating a lot more and retaliating in really vicious ways, to the point where sites get shut down, people drop off of sites," she said.

"It's like being behind a mask. It offers that sort of anonymous screen for a woman to say some things that she wouldn't normally say."

For us, it all started with a volunteer area rep for Dogs Deserve Better in the Seattle area, Kelly Page. Kelly was doing excellent work for chained dogs, and had received kudos for a case she brought to the public, a dog who was being mistreated and locked in a basement.

In fact, when the case broke and media covered their quest to save Lucky, Kelly was called up for jury duty that day. While there, a King County employee said, "Wait a second, are you Kelly Page from Dogs Deserve Better, the one who's saving Lucky?"

Kelly was shocked, and replied, "Yes, that's me."

The employees agreed, "Excuse her immediately. Go save Lucky, girl!" When Kelly stood up, her fellow jurors started clapping, applauding, and giving her hugs as she walked out of the courtroom. (Lucky would end up being returned to his cruel situation, as is so often the case.)

Soon, however, Kelly's doctor asked about her work for chained dogs, telling her, "I'm a big dog lover, too! Maybe I can get involved; do you need foster homes?"

Kelly, who like all rescuers was always in need of foster homes, was initially receptive. "Sure!" she said. "I'll let you know when we have dogs in need of help."

Suzanne did become a foster parent, but returned many of the fosters very quickly, forcing Kelly to scramble to find another placement. Then Suzanne fostered a pit bull named Joel for approximately two months.

During this time, a different local chained dog came to the group's attention. Kelly sent me the following message:

"We've checked on this dog; the guy is definitely involved in dog fighting. We gave him our number and he said he would talk to his family about relinquishing. We have also spoken to the neighbor who made the report and got all the info.

"Suzanne contacted the neighbor originally representing herself as DDB, saying we (DDB) would do whatever it takes to get the dog out of the situation. I spoke with the neighbor and she was crying for the dog and didn't understand why the dog is still there. Animal control has been called and says of course, 'no violations at this time.'"

Suzanne didn't accept that Kelly's hands were tied, and began a campaign of harassment against her for not freeing the dog. When you work for chained dogs, you quickly learn that unless the owner is willing to give the dog up to rescue, there is nothing more you can do—unless you want to steal the dog and face arrest. We failed about 85-90% of the time.

Dr. Fiala placed all the blame on Kelly. She was also thinking about adopting her foster dog Joel, but told Kelly, "I am very conflicted about him, I don't need another dog, but I love him very much, so I need to work that out."

PET ADOPTION CONTRACT

The Adopter agrees to adopt the following animal (hereinafter called "Animal") from Dogs Deserve Better:

Name/Breed____Joel____Pitbull_____ Age _1 ½_

Color/Markings____brindle____ Sex _male_

As Adopter, I agree to the following

1. To allow a representative of Dogs Deserve Better to visit my premises to insure the terms of this agreement have been kept;
2. The Animal will not be kept outdoors; – sometimes – he will occasionally be
3. The Animal will not be kept on a chain; outside in a kennel.
4. The Animal will be provided with adequate fresh food and water, clean, dry shelter when outside, and daily exercise;

When filling out the adoption forms, she altered the adoption contract to specify that she might keep him outside in a kennel, and also wrote that DDB could only visit him one time with pre-arranged notice.

Marie Belanger, who was our rep coordinator at the time, was consulted by the folks in Seattle as to how to proceed; she advised them to deny the adoption. When volunteers took Joel back and moved him to another foster home, Dr. Fiala went ballistic, upping the campaign of harassment against Kelly—her patient—posting her personal contact information online, and suing DDB in court for the dog.

Suzanne then created a Facebook page and a video to engender sympathy from strangers, and use "her army" to target Kelly, myself, and the organization. As DDB was and remained the sole legal owner of Joel, we prevailed on all fronts before the judge.

Because of the doctor's campaign, the chained dogs of Seattle never again received help from Dogs Deserve Better.

Kelly had poured her heart and soul into helping her local chained dogs, as her final rep report would attest to: "Amassed 52 volunteers, seven foster homes, raised food and monetary donations and rescued close to 40 dogs; garnered 2800 followers on Facebook, got the chaining bill to the Senate floor and had four major media stories on chained dogs."

All that energy and purpose for the dogs was now gone.

Kelly was forced to move, change her number, and get a restraining order against the doctor, too, on behalf of herself and her daughter. Because Fiala had likely violated doctor-patient confidentiality and ethics laws by accosting her patient—using information she'd gained as part of her practice—complaints were filed with the medical board.

Suzanne lost the case in court and was ordered to pay Kelly's attorney fees, mailing attorney Adam Karp a box of pennies and nickels for the $1768.00 owed him.

Based upon the petition, testimony, and case record, the court finds that the respondent committed unlawful harassment, as defined in RCW 10.14.080, and was not acting pursuant to any statutory authority, and **IT IS THEREFORE ORDERED THAT:**

✓	Respondent is RESTRAINED from making any attempts to keep under surveillance petitioner and any minors named in the table above. *including but not limited to*
✓	Respondent is RESTRAINED from making any attempts to contact petitioner and any minors named in the table above. *directly or indirectly by mail, telephone, email, social network*
✓	Respondent is RESTRAINED from entering or being within _1000 feet_ (distance) of petitioner's ☐ residence ☑ place of employment ☐ other: *text or by or through any third persons except legal ??*
✓	Judgment is granted against respondent for fees and costs in the amount of $ ~~1655.00~~
✓	Other: If both parties are in the same location, respondent shall leave. *$1,768.00*

After Kelly got the restraining order, Dr. Fiala switched her focus full-time onto Dogs Deserve Better and me as its founder. Since I'd never met her before and lived across the country, I had much less legal protection from her abuse and the lies she

IT WENT TO THE DOGS

spread.

The Washington state medical board subsequently forced her to undergo a psychiatric exam, upon the recommendation of a Dr. Neff, who said in part:

"Suzanne Fiala suffers from a mental health condition, which she herself describes to be a diagnosed Bipolar Disorder. . . . Individuals may become enraged over minor events. . . . They may exercise poor judgment and get into conflicts with others and the law. This is consistent with the campaign instigated and carried out by Dr. Fiala against Patient A in response to the denial of her dog adoption. Her steadfast insistence on blaming the patient for her predicament in the absence of any objective evidence that her patient was responsible is all quite consistent with a relapse. Her inability or unwillingness to recognize the effects of her actions on her patient is another example suggesting that her bipolar illness is not under adequate control. . . .

"There were also significant boundary violations of which Respondent seemed to be totally unaware. Her choice of paying her fine in small coins was a clear example of very poor judgment and detachment from the inappropriateness of such behavior towards the court and the law. . . .

"Her abrupt shift in her relationship and attitude towards Patient A . . . , her extreme tenacity and persistence in the face of legal and economic consequences to her, and her insensitivity to the effects on the patient are consistent with the existence of problematic personality traits and/or a personality disorder.

"The evidence in this case indicates actual harm to Patient A, whose life was significantly disrupted by Respondent's intrusive campaign against her and her family. . . . In my opinion, Dr. Fiala remains at risk of responding to others in her life, including patients, in a similar, inappropriate, and potentially harmful manner."

Although I'm unsure what the ordered evaluation uncovered or what was done as a result, I do know that Fiala gave up her private practice; I doubt that was done willingly. I have reason to believe that she used online aliases to continue her harassment against me and the organization after she was forced to curtail overt harassment for a period of time.

against Patient A is unlikely to be limited to one specific trigger. It is likely that Dr. Fiala will repeat her impaired behavior in other situations. Without a comprehensive, independent evaluation and a successful redesign of her psychiatric treatment regime, all her patients are at potential risk of harm.

Finally, withdrawal from practice and a comprehensive assessment also protect the physician, Dr. Fiala. Given that in a relapse she can neither adequately control her behavior nor perceive when she is behaving or thinking inappropriately, her present and future interests are best served by taking the above actions.

I declare, under penalty of perjury by the laws of the state of Washington, that the above is true and correct.

Signed at *Sisters, Oregon* (city & state) on this *13th* day of August, 2012.

Sisters, Oreg.   *Kent E. Neff*
KENT E. NEFF, MD, FAPA

Suzanne had expressed ambivalence about adopting a dog that put her over the legal limit of dogs in her neighborhood, changed our contract, and then attacked and vowed to destroy us when we decided against her adoption. She'd even admitted to manically collecting animals in an article she wrote about her bipolar disorder. "Before I sought consistent treatment, my manic times were too crazy. I recall looking at stuffed rabbits in a department store display and finding them so strangely appealing I felt compelled to buy six . . . I would get new pets from a shelter."

There is much talk today of the stigma associated with mental illness, but what of those whose mental illness specifically causes them to lash out and harm others? What about when that mental illness is used as an excuse for bad behavior? Is there no recourse for citizens who find themselves in the crosshairs and with no way out?

I was feeling the strain of all the attacks, and yet I had no choice but to continue to care for our dogs and do the work of the organization. If I went under, where would our dogs go? I couldn't bear to let them and our donors down.

I had to soldier on.

Heff chews on one of his Christmas gifts, alongside a note a school student wrote to him.

CHAPTER TWENTY-ONE:
Girl Scouts & Santa Paws Bring Hope for our Dogs, and Me

"You and the dogs surely tugged at the girls' hearts yesterday. I can't wait to talk to the girls about it. I know I told several people about our trip yesterday and the amazing work that you do."—Debbie S., troop leader

In December, as our first Christmas approached, a local girl scout troop came to visit, arranged and accompanied by troop leaders. They'd made toys, treats, and collected and brought donations of food and other goodies for the dogs, too.

This group of young ladies brought a huge smile to my face,

reminding me that even in the midst of chaos and trauma, there was still good in our world; our youth still needed grownups who could be positive role models for them. They gave me hope.

The girls played with and loved on the dogs for over two hours before reluctantly taking their leave, promises of more help to come trailing in their wake.

Each year at the holidays, DDB undertook a Santa Paws campaign, where we raised money to buy each of our foster dogs a Petco or Petsmart gift card; plus, our supporters mailed gifts to the dogs of their choice, too.

It was our first Christmas in our very own facility, and we were beyond excited, posting this to our supporters:

All the rescue dogs at the Good Newz Rehab Center have their own tiny stockings hung by the chimney with care. They eagerly await Santa, and will have a hard time sleeping in their tiny (and not so tiny) beds tonight, visions of toys and treats dancing through their heads.

Don't tell them, but there are 20 boxes of gifts just waiting for them come tomorrow morning. We can't wait to see how excited they will be!

They asked us to pass along a message to you all...THANK YOU, THANK YOU, THANK YOU! From the bottom of our hearts and theirs, for another extra special and successful sponsor year!

Each dog pictured on our page, 30 in all, from both the center and DDB foster homes, received gift packages from our donors and were sponsored online for gift cards. Santa Paws has matched our gifts up to $5000 again this year, and she popped the check in the mail this week.

If you celebrate Christmas, this is the season of love. Be kind to strangers, feed and rescue a stray dog, and give yourself all the love you deserve.

I'd say Polly had a bit of a kong fetish.

CHAPTER TWENTY-TWO:

Sick & Alone

Anew year was upon us, and in January and February of 2012, money at the center was very tight; Katie had quit, and I couldn't afford to hire another caretaker for the dogs. During that time, I did much of the dog care myself, working with as many as 14 dogs each day, and gratefully accepting volunteer help when I could get it.

Oddly enough, all the dogs survived, and dare I say even thrived, while many had been adopted and new dogs had taken their place.

It wasn't ideal, but I was doing my very best to make it work.

In March I took a $9,000 pay cut in order to push that money over to hiring at least one caretaker immediately.

During that time, I remember a weekend I was all alone at the center, with no volunteer help scheduled. I planned to make the best of it, except I came down with a bad case of the flu. Because of course I did.

I didn't just get a normal, everyday cold now, mind you. No, I came down with the full-blown "I'm dyin ova heyar" flu, complete with a temperature of 102.5, chills, headache, and vomiting. It was one of those "just let me croak" illnesses, one you wouldn't wish on your worst enemy.

Well, maybe one or two of them.

I've never been a person who handles fever well, and so at that temperature I was practically delirious and hallucinating.

My circumstances were dire, but I knew that not caring for the dogs wasn't an option. It would never be an option as long as I was breathing. So I pulled myself out of bed, sobbing all the while, and would have thrown myself the biggest pity party imaginable if I weren't too sick to bake a cake.

I did everything that needed to be done that morning, even walking the dogs in the field, because I knew they needed that energy release. Then I took the dogs I could trust with cats up into my room with me, and crated the rest for their safety, while I dragged myself back into bed for an hour or two.

I repeated this routine another couple of times throughout the day, making sure the dogs still got to run and play, still got their two square meals. For a two-day period I focused only on survival, for both myself and the animals. I didn't worry about emails, phone calls, Surry County, the bullying Washington doctor, or any of the other myriad problems facing the organization.

There's something about a crisis, when your world shrinks to just one pinpoint of light, that tends to put things into perspective. I knew that, for that one day, we would just do our best and move on. It would become a badge of honor for me, mostly for the fact that I made it through and so did the dogs.

Even though that flu was miserable, it now stands in my mind as one of the least horrible of the occurrences during the first two years at 1915 Moonlight Road.

Sugar in Pennsylvania trying to survive sub-zero windchills without food, water, or straw.

CHAPTER TWENTY-THREE:
A Happy Update on Sugar

*N*othing brightens an animal rescuer's day like a happy update from a pup they've freed. On the coldest day in the winter of 2010, I'd given food, water, and straw to two underweight dogs left shivering in the snow and with inadequate housing. I was subsequently charged with trespassing, but it would be one of the few cases I'd win in the end.

In a bizarre twist to the case, months later the caretakers called and asked me to take the dogs into rescue. I just couldn't believe my ears; were they trying to trick me into coming onto their property so they could charge me again? I was skeptical, and told him as much on the phone. He said, "I understand your position, however, we're being truthful. We've come to agree with you that the girls deserve a better life. Can you help?"

I immediately said "Yes!"—but agreed to meet them at a local park, just to be on the safe side.

Cinnamon and Sugar were dream fosters, and both ended up in absolutely lovely homes. The last day of my illness I awoke to this wonderful email in my inbox:

"We went sledding the other day in the yard (first time this year) and I had to forward a few pics of Sugar . . . do you see the big smile on her face? Thanks to you she is running like the wind and loving her life! I still view her YouTube video[*] and I cannot believe she lived chained up and pretty much ignored. I have never seen a dog run as fast as she does when she gets into the open field. I just like to send you an update, because you must know the work you do means everything to these dogs . . . you are appreciated."—Carrie Lamb

Sugar playing with "her boys" in the snow.

[*] View the video at https://youtu.be/iuzyIjlY4m8

The snow was melting, but they ran through the puddles anyway!

CHAPTER TWENTY-FOUR:

State Vet's Office Arrives for a "Friendly" Visit

"I WAS SO HAPPY TO HEAR THAT THE "HOUSE OF HORRORS" HAD BEEN PURCHASED BY A DOG RESCUE ORGANIZATION. IT WOULD BECOME A PLACE OF HEALING AND NEW LIFE FOR ABUSED AND NEGLECTED DOGS, AND I WANTED TO BE A PART OF IT IN SOME SMALL WAY. I BEGAN VOLUNTEERING ON WEEKENDS AND IT IS ONE OF THE MOST REWARDING THINGS I'VE EVER DONE. I FELL IN LOVE WITH EVERY DOG THERE, AND THEY ALL SEEMED TO KNOW THAT THEIR LIVES WERE CHANGING IN THE MOST WONDERFUL WAY. THEY WERE SHELTERED, FED AND LOVED, AND THEY WERE GRATEFUL."—LESLIE THIBEAULT, VOLUNTEER

*I*n January of 2012, the state vet's office showed up for the first—but not the last—time. It turned out we were supposed to "get approval" from them before starting a shelter, something we hadn't known about. As I'd understood it, obtaining the county kennel license was our only requirement, but it looked like I was wrong.

"OK, then," I asked. "How do we fix it?"

We'd been very public about our efforts, and there were tons of articles and interviews, both before and after we moved to the location. It certainly wasn't like we were hiding anything. Wouldn't it make sense for the state vet's office to proactively contact us—or anyone they learned was set to open a shelter—to educate us about the requirements and help us get started?

But this didn't happen. It would be months before they would darken our door and the inspector, Sherry Helsel, and her co-worker walked the property, exploring every shed and kennel that was owned by Vick—and unused by us, as our dogs lived inside the home.

I would later find out that she photographed these dirty and disgusting areas and reported them to her supervisor as if we kept our dogs there. I was shocked!

The last we heard from Ms. Helsel was via e-mail the next month, in which she told us to add our figures to the required online reports, and she would be in touch as far as our approval went. Six months would pass before they'd show up again.

From: "Helsel, Sheryl (VDACS)"
Subject: Dogs Deserve Better Custody Records
Date: Mon, Feb 13, 2012 2:39 pm

"You should definitely submit a report for 2011, it is due by 2/15, and will be a violation if submitted after that time. I am reviewing the custody records, and will contact you regarding compliance in that area, as well as the process of approving the facility. Thank you for your cooperation."

Lucy was a sweet girl forced to live in a pen, but given up to DDB with her sister Emma.

CHAPTER TWENTY-FIVE:

Sabotaged from Within

"WE ARE LEFT IN SHOCK BECAUSE WE WEREN'T PREPARED, SO WE JUST SHAKE OUR HEADS AND SAY THE SAME THING: 'I NEVER SAW THAT COMING. HOW COULD THEY DO THAT?' BUT DON'T FEEL BAD ABOUT NOT HAVING A NATURAL ABILITY TO SEE THEM COMING. IF YOU DON'T HAVE LARCENY IN YOUR HEART, IT'S VERY HARD TO RECOGNIZE THAT MINDSET IN OTHERS."
—DR. PHIL, "LIFE CODE: NEW RULES FOR THE REAL WORLD"

*D*eana had to be a sociopath.

It's the only thing that makes sense to me now, but at the time I didn't see it or have a clue.

According to Martha Stout in *The Sociopath Next Door*[6], every sociopath is different, and their motivation is different, just like people with other personality disorders, or your average "normal" citizen. Some sociopaths do illegal things for kicks, some out of desperation, and some just enjoy the thrill of destroying others. All sociopaths lack a conscience, the ability to feel shame, and so are freed from social norms to do whatever they'd like.

I've spent years pondering what happened to me and the organization, and trying to understand why Deana behaved as she did; the only reasonable conclusion I can come to is that she's sociopathic in nature, DDB and I were her targets, and it was all one big game.

In fact, I'd be more than willing to bet she's running a similar scam on some other unsuspecting victim at this very moment. God help them.

If you asked Deana today if she deliberately set out to harm me or DDB, she would deny it up and down, and proclaim certain innocence while batting her eyelashes and smiling sweetly. She would say that she still has the "upmost" respect for me and the organization, and she certainly never stole any money.

She has a bible verse tattooed on her foot, for goodness sake. Of course she's innocent!

Yet, the evidence shows that she was responsible for payroll and the theft was incontrovertible: she was directly padded her paycheck for four months before quitting. If one were so inclined as to give her the benefit of the doubt, rest assured that no one else's paycheck mysteriously (and incrementally) increased during that time.

It's my personal conclusion (feel free to draw your own) that Deana wasn't a criminal mastermind, but she COULD make trouble from behind the scenes and make her exit stage left as things fell apart in her wake. In *The Sociopath Next Door*, Stout states, "Maybe you cannot be the CEO of a multinational corporation, but you can frighten a few people, or cause them to scurry around like chickens, or steal from them, or—maybe best of all—create situations that make them feel bad about themselves. And this is power, especially when the people you manipulate are superior to you in some way. . . . This is not only good fun; it is existential vengeance. And without a conscience, it is amazingly easy to do."

When I read that paragraph, a lightbulb went off in my head. THAT was Deana, to a T. And it was exactly what she'd done to me and the organization she claimed to "love."

By April, Deana had started to make as much trouble as she could in order to distract from her own crimes. Given the corruption at the Commonwealth Attorney's office, she was relatively assured it would work.

Pay Period: 02/19/2012 - 03/03/2012 Direct Deposit

Employee
Deana B Whitfield

Earnings and Hours	Qty	Rate	Current	YTD Amount
Salary	1:00		767.97	3,670.92

Pay Period: 03/04/2012 - 03/17/2012 Direct Deposit

Employee
Deana B Whitfield·

Earnings and Hours	Qty	Rate	Current	YTD Amount
Salary	1:00		1,005.54	4,676.46

Pay Period: 03/18/2012 - 03/31/2012 Direct Deposit

Employee
Deana B Whitfield

Earnings and Hours	Qty	Rate	Current	YTD Amount
Salary	1:00		1,023.08	5,699.54

Pay Period: 06/10/2012 - 06/23/2012 Direct Deposit

Employee
Deana B Whitfield

Earnings and Hours	Qty	Rate	Current	YTD Amount
Salary	1:00		1,053.00	10,844.86

Cocker Spaniel Baylee in the pen. "Please get me outta here!"

CHAPTER TWENTY-SIX:
She Called Us Crying About Her Dogs

I loved hands-on rescue work, and that spring I was blessed to finally get involved again. Since we'd moved to Virginia and opened our doors, we'd been so inundated with requests for help from our reps and citizens alike that we'd had very little time to get out into our new community and help local dogs.

But that changed when a woman from Suffolk called and spoke to us about her pups, crying all the while. Baylee, 7, and Nala, 9, had lived inside with her most of their lives, until she met and started a family with her current partner. Now she had an 8-week-old baby, and Nala and Baylee hadn't seen the inside of a home in months.

When Nala injured herself trying to escape the pen she

shared with the tiny blonde cocker, the caller finally realized life outside and ostracized from the family was no life for her once-valued family members.

With tears in her eyes, but knowing it was the right thing to do, she signed over ownership of the dogs to Dogs Deserve Better.

I felt badly both for her and the dogs that they would lose one another, but I agreed that life in a pen was unacceptable. The woman, who I believe genuinely loved the dogs, came to visit them once after they arrived at our center. She left very upset, telling me it was too hard to see them. "I won't be back, I just can't; but I want to thank you for giving them the love and home I no longer can."

Nala breathed a sigh of relief to be back living inside the home where she belonged.

Nala would forever after suffer extreme anxiety during thunderstorms, but she and Baylee quickly remembered their housetraining and inside manners, and soon were off into the brighter futures they deserved.

Anthony carried his toy everywhere with him, even in the field.

CHAPTER TWENTY-SEVEN:
Anthony is Attacked

In April, our sweet Anthony was attacked on a field run by two of our other center dogs, Jada and Copper. I wasn't out there at the time, dog caretaker Zeko was, but thank God I was onsite that weekend. Zeko called me from his cell phone, and since English isn't his first language and he was frantically yelling, I couldn't understand a word he said—but I knew it had to be bad. I thought either he was being attacked, or one of the dogs was.

I was in a panic, and instead of wisely opening the gate and driving the van out to the field, I started running out instead. It quickly became obvious that I was out of shape (as if I didn't know that already), and by the time I got to where he was with the dogs, I was panting and stumbling. Zeko had gotten the dogs off of Anthony by hitting them with a nearby tree branch, and was standing protectively over the injured dog while he waited for help.

I wish I could claim to be the calm one in an emergency, but I typically freak out first, then get myself together and do what needs to be done. I was terrified to approach, terrified to ask: who was attacked? Was the dog alive?

It turned out it was poor little Anthony, and he was ripped up. I never took photos of him in that state, because it hurt so much I never wanted to see it again. But the memory of it is seared into my brain, and the pain I felt upon seeing this sweet sweet dog laying there with gashes all over him almost destroyed me.

Needless to say, Zeko was really shook up too; we were both a mess.

Zeko had been a hero, though; he'd saved a life.

It was a Saturday morning, and the vets' offices were either closed or had shortened hours. I lifted Anthony into the van and rushed him straight to the nearest vet that we used—Rogers in the nearby town of Smithfield—praying they were still open. I couldn't stop shaking, and I cry even now as I remember the story.

The doctor and staff jumped into action, and the people who were due to go in next gladly offered up their spot for Anthony to get the emergency treatment he needed. They started an IV, took xrays, and checked his vitals, and then sent us with his IV fluids to an emergency clinic where he could get the 24/7 care he needed.

Anthony would survive his ordeal, spending days at the vet until he was well enough to come home. We were lucky: our boy could have lost his life.

This served as a reminder to us to take very seriously the harm dogs are capable of doing to one another, and consider ways we could better ensure both the safety of our dogs and our staff.

Within just a few months, Anthony got his forever home in New Jersey, where he would live a wonderful and much-loved life as a valued family member. His mom sent photos and pup-dates many times over the next few years.

Jada and Copper would never get a chance again to be part of the bigger pack; they spent the rest of their time at the center as a little pack of two, or with one other member of the opposite sex—for safety's sake.

Anthony visits the beach in New Jersey.

Jada and Copper, exploring the field together.

Eva and Lindsay were forced to both live in one crate, outside.

CHAPTER TWENTY-EIGHT:
Two Dogs, One Crate

The call came in asking for help for two dogs living in a crate outside in Hampton, Virginia. The young woman had moved a month before, and now (if the dogs were lucky) she drove by once a day to give them food, water, and a potty break. We assumed the caller actually meant a kennel and not a crate, but upon arrival Deana was appalled; two eight-month-old puppies were crammed into a single crate—in a shed, with garbage and old tools surrounding them—without a drop of food or water in sight.

When Deana freed them from the crate, both dogs immediately starting licking the grass for any available moisture. The woman asked, "Why are they doing that?" She didn't even understand that THEY WERE THIRSTY!

As the center was full, our intention was to assess the situation and seek a foster home; when Deana texted me a picture of the horrendous conditions, we immediately pulled them out—not another day would be spent cramped in that crate!

Eva and Lindsay would now know the joy of being dogs. They would learn to play again, and even find a foster home where they napped on the bed and were cuddled daily.

Both girls quickly and easily got the loving homes they deserved, and we got to make a difference in a dog's life. I'd definitely call that a win.

The girls sleep together on the bed in their foster home.

Eva and Lindsay running in the front yard at the center.

One of my favorite center photos.

CHAPTER TWENTY-NINE:
Department of Labor

The first action Deana took to create chaos and throw us off her scent was to report us to the Department of Labor. I assume this was also done to get even with me, because she'd been missing so much work that I moved her pay to hourly instead of salaried.

Deana was salaried at 35 hours per week, working five hours a day onsite and supposedly two hours a day from home. She claimed she'd been diagnosed with MS (never showing any proof of such), and that she was going to medical appointments during the days she missed. She never offered to make up the hours.

If she weren't padding her paycheck AND if she worked all her hours, this wouldn't have resulted in any lesser income. But if she WERE doing something illegal, then this would put a damper on her activities.

I'll be honest; although Deana was (and probably still is) quite diabolical, I'm not convinced she was a very wise criminal. I say this because she would tell different agencies conflicting stories, depending upon where their avenue of focus was.

She didn't seem concerned at all about her stories matching up.

Whatever would cause a particular agency to take action against us, she'd tell them.

Case in point: she went to the Department of Labor and told them that our facility was a dangerous place to work, because the dogs were left uncaged and therefore employees were receiving severe bite and other related injuries.

This claim was easily disproven by the fact that there were no hospital or doctor reports of dog bites from our facility, not only from that time-frame, but from the entire four years I would be there. Any injury that is serious enough to warrant stitches or other medical care automatically triggers a report to the state and local authorities, who come calling to ensure the dog is quarantined or put down, according to the severity of the situation.

Perhaps Deana didn't know that serious bites are reported; or, more likely she didn't care that it was immediately disproven—just that she could stir up the trouble.

To be sure, we'd had a few "nips" or incidental scratches, but there had been nothing serious as far as humans go. The attack on Anthony was the most serious incident that occurred on my watch, and I'd be happy to never repeat the experience again.

Making the exact opposite claim, she would later tell the local animal control that our dogs were caged 24/7, and this confinement was cruel and inhumane on my part.

To anyone who would study the pieces to this puzzle, it quickly becomes obvious that we couldn't both be allowing our dogs to run the countryside willy nilly AND keeping them confined in tiny cages for their entire lives.

The complaint with the Department of Labor came through anonymously, as I suppose such things do, and Deana ran around "helping" me address the issues raised in the report. That she made up.

I can picture her snickering to herself all the while.

She didn't admit that it was her, of course, for quite awhile, not until I publicly put out the evidence of her embezzling—but she did eventually brag about doing it online. While at the same time insisting, of course, that she meant me and DDB no ill will.

 Deana Whitfield

1. Filed first complaint with the Dept of Va Osha on 5/21/12.

2. Fell at work 5/2012 and dislocated my knee and DID NOT report to Workman Comp but instead paid through my insurance because DDB did not need an extra bill.

3. Reported to ACO a week before I gave my letter of resignation and my last day of work of 6/26/2012.

Deana also asked me to buy Halt Dog pepper spray for the protection of the staff, which, after Anthony's attack, I wasn't opposed to. Zeko had had to use a tree branch to save Anthony, and it seems that pepper spray would be a safer and kinder alternative if a staff member found him/herself in such a situation again.

I was ultimately responsible for both the safety of our dogs and our employees, yet we were working every single day with dogs who'd lived chained for life. This meant there was always a greater chance they would have aggression issues—a 3X greater chance, in fact, according to the CDC. These dogs weren't socialized with other dogs or humans, and—like all animals—they could be unpredictable.

Staff needed to both be aware of these risks and come up with and train in ways to protect human and animal life if a crisis arose. I believed that the dog pepper spray would be a good last line of defense, and so I ordered a 12-pack of it.

Note in the following email, Deana tells me "this is the brand I have."

From: <office@dogsdeservebetter.org>
Subject: **This is the brand I have-Dog spray**
Date: June 4, 2012 at 10:40:08 AM EDT

http://www.magidglove.com/Halt-Dog-Repellent-12-Box-AR61101.aspx

A box of 12 isn't that expensive.

Deana Whitfield
Dogs Deserve Better Inc.

We'd bought a couple single cans of it by her request, but soon realized the product would be useless if not within reach of a staff member during an attack. In purchasing a 12-pack, each dog caretaker could carry one in his/her staff pouch (which contained dog treats for training, a first aid kit, and anything else the staff member deemed important).

We also placed one in every room, out of the dogs' reach, where staff could easily grab it in case of emergencies.

These items were treated the same way one treats a fire extinguisher, and staff was alerted that they were to be used only as a last resort to save lives.

We also had the stun gun Joe had bought me (for protection from human assailants) in the kitchen, and he'd added a smaller one that could be used as a last resort in dog attacks, too.

It's an unfortunate fact that dogs can and do attack and kill humans. In 2011 and 2012, dogsbite.org claims that "70 dog attacks resulted in human death: there were 32 child victims and 38 adult victims" for the two-year period.

The last thing I wanted was one of my staff to be killed by a dog, but I also understood there were certain risks that came with our job. I believed then, and I still believe now, that any-one who isn't willing to take those risks shouldn't be in the dog rescue business.

We were also facing persistent misconceptions on the part of the dog-loving public who *wasn't* involved in the day to day world of rescue: specifically, that all dogs are cute little fuzzy lovebugs who would never hurt a fly.

Believe me, I wish that were the case; it would have made my life much, much easier.

The truth, like most truths, is somewhere in the middle. I've pulled dogs off chains who were from the get-go the sweetest, most loving dogs you could ever imagine. Then I removed a dog from a chain who tried to kill me in my kitchen.

Most dogs are more than capable of learning and growing toward a place of trust with both humans and other dogs in a very short amount of time, making wonderful and loving family companions.

Unfortunately, not every dog will.

It was our job at the center to give each dog who came to us a chance, help them with the socialization and training they needed to succeed inside a family unit, and adopt them out for a happily ever after.

In order to accomplish this task, crating or caging our dogs 24/7 was out of the question. Not only is it cruel, but it certainly doesn't teach a dog how to live inside with the family, or how to get along with other dogs and humans.

Freedom and interaction, as well as play and exercise, were necessities.

Those who didn't understand the risks or looked for a way to shame us for doing our best had no business working in the rescue world.

On May 23rd, I received the following email from Deana, in her guise as "helping" me against whatever scallywag had the nerve to file a report with the Department of Labor. I left most of the spelling errors:

Here are a few things I noticed on other shelter sites etc. Ask her do we need these as well?

1. MSDS sheets - these are to list like clorox, laundry soap and what other "chemicals" we have and proper use of them for the employees

2. Safety training for - wet floors from moping, proper hand washing after handling a dog, dog meds and food and proper techniques for animal fights etc.

3. Lyme Dis. - Do we have to discuss this with employees since they walk in fields and teach them proper use of freaking bug spray? *[Her disgust here is kinda funny. How dare they!]*

4. Evacuation plan - Do we have to have a written evac plan for animals and employees?

5. PPE - thats the protective gear shit we were talking about like catch poles or something

6. Proper disposal of waste (dog shit) and proper clean up of crate ect. Like wearing golves ect.

7. Clearly marked exit signs on all exits

I figure we should just handle all these to keep us clear from any more calls. *[So very kind of her to look out for us like this!]* If you can think of anything else, I think we should try and cover even the things that are common sense.

Deana creates a mess, and laughs while she watches me stress and worry about how to fix it.

That is one very sick human.

The Department of Labor closed our case.

Cowboy's family joins me at the Massachusetts Capitol. They even made their own sign.

CHAPTER THIRTY:

Chain Off 2012

*B*y that June we had enough staffing in place for me to start doing some activist work again. Deana was still office manager, plus we had two dog caretakers, Andrea Wheeler and Zeko, plus another part-time staff member who helped with cleaning two hours a day.

I left to do a nine-state tour, wherein I chained myself to doghouses in front of state Capitol buildings in Connecticut, Maryland, Massachusetts, New Hampshire, New Jersey, New York, Pennsylvania, Rhode Island, and Virginia. All told, that year we had 46 people nationwide who chained with the dogs (and me) in hopes of a better world.[*]

I wrote the following while sitting on my chain that June:

---

[*] Video footage http://youtu.be/DiSxONYnxeA

Imagine . . . a World without Chains

Not too long ago a supporter said to me "We aren't making a difference for chained dogs. Things are the same as they always were."

I thought about it for a minute, and then I said **"That's not my reality."**

Instead of seeing our glass as overturned, empty, I invite you to see our glass as filling with all the beauty we desire to see happen in our world. **I'd like to inspire you to Imagine with me a world without chains, because that's where real truth begins; in our imaginations.**

Only as we can imagine greater things can we start to believe in them. Only when we can spend even a moment of every day seeing what CAN be instead of what MAY be in this moment, can we start moving toward the picture of love and perfection we hold in our minds.

Only when we believe it can happen do we start taking inspired action to bring it forth into our experience.

Can you imagine what it would feel like to know that every dog in your community is safe and loved? Can you imagine a day where you wake up in the morning overflowing with confidence and a certainly that all is well for every canine in your neighborhood?

What would you do to celebrate your freedom from the chains of despair you've been carrying for so long?

How would you celebrate the realization that your burden was no longer there, that you too were FREE to be happy, FREE to be loved, FREE to be joyous and FREE to be—most of all— F R E E ?

Ten years ago I started Dogs Deserve Better, because I dreamed of a world without chains. I believed dogs deserved better than life on a chain and I passionately embraced ways to bring them this freedom.

I've faced down many giants in the path to winning them freedom, and I've lost my way in the desert of despair. I've been overwhelmed by the need, besieged by the guilt, and overrun by the hatred, until a point where I could hardly breathe under the thick cloud of desperation I carried on my shoulders.

But not today.

Today I imagine, today I believe, and today I dream.

Today I will continue to build our facility for chained dogs, because there I see my dreams come true. I see dogs who suffered so greatly learn to love and allow love to come into their world. I see them earn their place amongst the stars who believe they are worthy of a great home and a great family.

Chained in front of the New York State Capitol in Albany.

This year as I chain myself to a doghouse in their stead, I imagine the day man opens his heart to the cruelty and releases Our Best Friends from this insane bondage. As I travel to nine state capitol buildings, trundle out my doghouse and heavy tow chain, endure heat, bugs, indifference, and ridicule, I pray for a miracle, that my inspired action may warm the heart of the right legislator, that my deed touches the soul of more than my compatriots, and that an arrow of knowledge is shot straight to the spirit of mankind.

I Imagine a World without Chains. I hope you'll join me.

Ah, fun in Florida, while they plot your demise elsewhere.

CHAPTER THIRTY-ONE:

Deana is Discovered, and Surry County Animal Control Shows Up

"SIMPLY PUT, I GOT CONNED. SHE KNEW WHAT WAS IMPORTANT TO ME; SHE PUSHED WHAT SHE KNEW WOULD RESONATE WITH MY VALUE SYSTEM. I IGNORED MY INSTINCTS AND GAVE HER THE BENEFIT OF THE DOUBT. I THOUGHT THAT WAS 'THE THING TO DO.' BUT IN THE REAL WORLD, WHERE YOU AND I ACTUALLY LIVE, IT SIMPLY ALLOWED THAT WOLF IN SHEEP'S CLOTHING TO PULL THE WOOL RIGHT OVER MY EYES."—DR. PHIL, "LIFE CODE: NEW RULES FOR THE REAL WORLD"

*J*oe finished his Afghanistan deployment that July, and we took the first of two vacations we'd planned to celebrate our honeymoon and the start of our lives together as a married couple. We'd been married over a year by now, but had barely seen one another; we would joke that our first year had exceeded our expectations—we hardly fought at all!

We flew to Miami and then drove down to the Florida Keys, just taking a few days to relax . . . something we both sorely needed. He'd worked 12-hour shifts the whole four months he was in Afghanistan, but yet we'd both agreed that maybe my year had been worse.

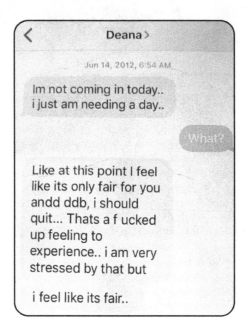

> **< Deana >**
>
> Jun 14, 2012, 6:54 AM
>
> Im not coming in today..
> i just am needing a day..
>
> What?
>
> Like at this point I feel like its only fair for you andd ddb, i should quit... Thats a f ucked up feeling to experience.. i am very stressed by that but
>
> i feel like its fair..

Deana had quit (again) the month before, stressing it was "only right because she missed so much work"; and a local woman, Melissa Wischmeier, had taken over the office manager position. While Deana was training Melissa to run payroll, she took the new girl outside for a smoke break, then told her she had to go to the bathroom.

Deana went back inside and ran her paycheck herself, which raised a red flag with Melissa.

She began to investigate.

When Melissa subsequently took over the office@dogsde-servebetter.org e-mail account, she hadn't thought to change the password. Deana continued to get the DDB e-mails sent to her on her phone, unbeknownst to any of us.

This meant that when I responded to Melissa's email about Deana stealing money on July 15th, Deana was among the first to know we were onto her. By the next morning, Deb, our treasurer, had an e-mail from Deana that revealed that she knew that we knew that she'd embezzled our funds.

Even though I quickly figured out what happened and went into the e-mail account to change the password, the damage had been done.

Since the money was so easily taken without our knowledge or permission, DDB corrected our oversight and started doing payroll online; it was then checked by the treasurer or me each pay cycle. No one else's pay deviated from the norm during this time frame, and Deana demonstrated at numerous points that she was aware what she was supposed to be paid.

I would also find out from the treasurer that Deana hadn't done much if any of the bookkeeping that was part of her job since she took over from Elaine.

I now believe she probably didn't even know HOW to do bookkeeping, as she'd claimed. I felt like such a fool.

On July 20th, while Joe and I were on vacation in Florida, local animal control officer Tracy Terry showed up on our doorstep for the first time.

I would later learn that Deana had been conspiring with one of our dog caretakers, Andrea Wheeler, which meant that of course Tracy Terry showed up while Andrea was working instead of Zeko.

Melissa called me immediately to let me know that animal control had been at the facility, and I'm sure were I there I probably would have been stupid enough to allow them in, too. Transparency and all that.

But I've since learned that when dealing with an unfriendly animal control (which we were), they don't get to step foot on your property without a warrant.

Why give them time to plant evidence or do other nefarious things?

Tracy Terry was fishing for something to be wrong, and I'm

frankly surprised that Andrea didn't engineer something for her to find. She did come during naptime, conveniently, which was between 2-4 p.m., and the dogs were in their crates sleeping at the time.

When I texted Andrea to see how it went, she was very nonchalant about it.

Me (aka dumbass): You doing ok? I heard animal control was there.

Andrea: Yeah I am fine. Yes, they stopped by Melissa and I gave them a tour.

[All sounds very innocent, doesn't it?]

Me: Did it seem to go ok in your opinion?

Andrea: I think so. The only thing she said was about the dogs being out in the heat and in the crate and I said we do the crate rotation and she made a note of that.

Me: So I wonder what they say to all the hunters with dogs in tiny cages 24/7 lol.

In truth, our dogs lived incredible lives compared to any of the dogs in that county who were forced to live in outside cages and kennels, and the animal control knew it.

But the truth didn't matter.

Joe and I on our St. Lucia honeymoon.

CHAPTER THIRTY-TWO:

Honeymoon, a Police Report, and Another Surprise Visit

"IT'S ABSOLUTELY IMPERATIVE THAT YOU DEVELOP AN URGENT AWARENESS OF WHO THESE PEOPLE ARE BECAUSE THEY ARE DANGEROUS TO BE AROUND. THEY CAN GET YOU IN TROUBLE JUST BY YOUR BEING IN THE WRONG PLACE AT THE WRONG TIME. EVEN WORSE, THE RULES THEY BREAK CAN BE IN THEIR INTERACTIONS WITH YOU BECAUSE YOU BECOME AN UNWITTING TARGET."—DR. PHIL, "LIFE CODE: NEW RULES FOR THE REAL WORLD"

During the next month, I was busy with organizational outreach, speaking and running a booth at the Animal Rights conference in DC, and was onsite only nine times at the same time as Deana's co-conspirator, dog caretaker Andrea Wheeler.

Dog caretaker Zeko had left to take a new job soon after animal control came by in July, and I'd hired three new caretakers, giving us four people for dog care instead of two.

Zeko's letter of resignation was clear evidence that we indeed treated our dogs well.

Zeko was from India, near the China border, and as such he'd had a very different relationship with animals where he lived than people in the U.S. do. He touched on that in his letter:

"It has been such a blessing to work with Dogs Deserve Better. If it weren't for my experience at your organization, I never would have realized the human responsibility to care for the animals God created. There is a vast gap between the way animals are treated in my home in India and how they are loved here. At times I was overwhelmed by the difference, but overall I enjoyed the experience."

Does this sound like a letter from someone witnessing or taking part in cruelty in any way? Hardly. In fact, it's quite the opposite, he openly admits to being overwhelmed by the care given to each of the dogs at the facility.

Zeko would later come back to work with the organization part time, and in fact he's the only original employee who still works at the Good Newz Rehab Center today.

To inject a spot of humor into a mostly humorless rehashing, I have a favorite memory about training Zeko how to care for the animals. We kept our dog food in the garage, and soon the mice were beating a path to our doorstep looking for some handouts. On top of taking measures to keep them out of the food using plastic garbage cans and bins, we also needed to catch and remove any who wandered onsite. I didn't want to kill them, because they're cute little guys who deserved to live too, so I bought humane traps instead of ones that kill.

After I went through the whole explanation with Zeko about how to use the traps and how they needed to be checked a couple of times each day, he nodded his head like he understood.

Then he said, "Ma'am, just one question. When we get this mouse inside, how do we kill it?"

I still laugh about it today. I started over, explaining that we didn't want to kill the mice, that was the whole reason for the humane traps—we needed to capture them and drive them far away, letting them loose in a field where there were no houses nearby.

It quickly became obvious that Deana had no intention of just quietly repaying the money she'd taken. She acted innocent, played stupid, and in the end just flat out refused to sign the letter of repayment.

Knowing now that she'd stolen our money, my mind was even more blown that she'd asked me for another job with the organization—twice!—since quitting on June 14th.

> No I totally get that, like 100%.. if there were any coord jobs open, that would be awesome but the office, i know what you are totally saying thats why

---

Subject: Hey
Date: June 18, 2012 at 1:34:51 PM EDT
To: Tami

Things are going good with Melissa...

We were chatting and she mentioned if I didn't quit she was our database girl when computer comes in, which I knew and she was looking forward to wirking with.. NOW, what I didn't know is she was going to be able to work from home with the database.. So, I was wondering if that is a position I could have?? I know my position with the office from my MS was to much but why can't I have another accomidating position due to my disability?

Deana Whitfield
Office Manager
Dogs Deserve Better Inc.
757.357.9292

Apparently, all that was to come was both my "punishment" for not allowing her another position with the organization, and discovering her embezzlement of our money.

Admittedly, there is a delicious irony to the fact that I took a paycut in order to afford more staff to care for the dogs, and Deana just helped herself to a chunk of it. If it hadn't happened to me, I might find it amusing.

```
VA0900000 Surry County Sheriff's Office

------------------- CFS REPORT# 2012-003940 -----------------------
CALL TYPE: 100-31 PAPER SERVICE          AGENCY: 4-SHERIFF
DISPATCHER: C858-Collier,Elizabeth C     RECEIVED:08/15/2012 12:47
JURISDICTION: 181-Surry                  HOW RECEIVED: 5-Sighted
DISPOSITION: 08-Referred to Another      ACTIVITY: 4-See Complaint
------------------------- COMPLAINANTS -----------------------------
TYPE          NAME                       PHONE          PID
COMPLAINANT   DOGS DERSERVE BETTER                      00516922
COMPLAINANT   THAYNE,TAMIRA C                           00514949
SUSPECT       WHITFIELD-JULIAN,DEANA                    00516923
--------------------------- ADDRESSES ------------------------------
CALLER  001915   MOONLIGHT                RD
OCCURRED 001915  MOONLIGHT                RD
----------------------------- UNITS --------------------------------
UNIT  AGENCY RECV  DISPATCH  ENROU ARRIV  TRANSPORT  CLRD  RETURN
                   ALRM1 ALRM2            ENROU ARRIV       STATION
10    SHERIFF 12:47 12:48     12:48                  13:29
      Referred to Another Agenc
--------------------------- COMMENTS -------------------------------
Dispatcher:C858@08/15/2012 13:23:04
MS. THAYNE CAME TO THE OFFICE TO OBTAIN PAPERWORK FOR EMBEZZLEMENT TO A NON PROFIT
ORGANIZATION.
SHE ADVISED THAT AN EMPLOYEE THAT NO LONGER WORKS THERE EMBEZZLED MONEY FROM THIS
ORGANIZATION. THIS HAPPENED OVER A 5 MONTH PERIOD. THE SUSPECT WAS GIVING HERSELF RAISES
DURING THAT TIME.
BASE GAVE THE CALL TO UNIT 10 (BACK).
THE CASE WILL BE TURNED OVER TO VIRGINIA STATE POLICE
Dispatcher:S910@08/31/2012 15:54:22
COPY OF THIS SCREEN LEFT IN AN ENVELOPE WITH DISP FOR DEANA WHITFIELD-JULIAN TO PICK UP
(PER DISP COLLIER, SHERIFF CLAYTON STATED IT WAS OKAY FOR HER TO HAVE A COPY)
Dispatcher:G739@09/19/2012 16:31:29
ON 9/19/12 MS. DEANA JULIAN-WHITFIELD CAME TO THE OFFICE AND A COPY OF THIS INCIDENT WAS
GIVEN TO HER PER U-1 (CLAYTON).
```

On August 15th, new office manager Melissa and I drove to the Surry County Sheriff's Office to file a police report. At the station I met with a Deputy Back about filing embezzlement charges against our former office manager. He told me that Whitfield had already called him and told him that if Dogs Deserve Better came in to file a police report, that we were lying, it was just a labor dispute.

He told me, "This is a red flag when the person accused of a crime calls in first. I had no idea what she was talking about, but I'm not surprised to see you here." We sat down and showed him our evidence, and he later called me back and told me he was turning the case over to the Virginia state police, as they had officers who specialized in embezzling cases.

Just before I left to drive to Joe's on August 17th in preparation for our flight to St. Lucia the next day, Andrea Wheeler came into the center and quit, saying she'd work the day but she wouldn't be coming back after that.

She seemed very stressed and nervous, but I put it down to being upset over her dilemma. "I had a big fight with my boyfriend, and I need to get out of town, move to Florida to be with my family. I'm sorry," she told me.

I was confused, but I never for a second thought it had anything to do with her conspiring with Deana. I was completely clueless.

I hugged her and told her I hoped that everything would work out for her, wishing her well. She would later send in a note with some items she was returning. In the note she says "You guys keep up the good work."

How many times are too many to use the term "dumbass" with regards to my naivete? I hugged her and wished her the best—all the while she was plotting to destroy me and my organization with the woman who was embezzling our money?

Deana had apparently figured her for the patsy who would do all the dirty work, while Deana sat back behind the scenes laughing, as she had all along.

Andrea may have foiled Deana's plan with her escape.

Although I tried hard to ignore the center for the week we were away—Joe requested I not look at emails or anything online—I had a feeling of dread hanging over my head the entire time.

I had difficulty focusing on relaxing and enjoying life while so much was going wrong back home. Even though I tried to chisel a smile on my face and heart—since his hard work overseas paid for our honeymoon—I knew he could see through my poor attempts, and it made me feel bad.

By the end of our week in St. Lucia, animal control would show up at our facility again, this time accompanied by the state vet's office.

Jay and Marley play ball in the field. Photo by Rita Thomas.

CHAPTER THIRTY-THREE:
Here We Go Again

"WHEN I BEGAN WORKING AS A CARETAKER AT DDB, I WAS SUFFERING TO THE POINT OF SELF-DESTRUCTION AND NEEDED JUST A GLIMMER OF HOPE. IN THE MONTHS TO FOLLOW I, TOO, BEGAN TO RECOVER THROUGH THE MUTUAL UNCONDITIONAL LOVE AND TRUST SHARED BETWEEN THOSE WOUNDED BEINGS AND MYSELF. SOME OF THE BEST DAYS OF MY LIFE UNFOLDED AND WERE EXPERIENCED IN A PLACE WHICH TAMI HAD REDEEMED FROM HOPELESSNESS, UNSPEAKABLE HORROR, PAIN, AND SUFFERING."—JAY GUNN, STAFF MEMBER

Once again, Tracy Terry would arrive while I was on vacation. Coincidence? I think not.

This time she brought along with her the state vet's official, Dan Kovich, who spent all day at our facility, ripping through our records and asking staff hundreds of questions. The employees were all forced to stay on premises while he was there—even those whose shift was done—which ended up costing the organization overtime pay in addition to the harassment and stress staff was subjected to.

Mind you, we'd been onsite at 1915 Moonlight Road for a year by this point. And they were just now deciding that we were somehow defective, after never taking more than a few minutes to enlighten us as to what they expected?

It's mindblowing to think that there used to be more than 55 pit bulls chained up in the back of this very same property, but now the mere fact that there were 12 dogs housed INSIDE THE BUILDING was somehow cause for great concern and upheaval on the part of officials.

To this day I still don't get it.

When I arrived at the center that Monday, I looked over our footage from outside the house. We had cameras set up in three locations, and I could clearly see Tracy Terry and Dan Kovich walking back to where the sheds and Vick's outdoor kennels were located, as if hoping against hope we were using them for our own dogs.

I'm sure they were disappointed to find a decided lack of living beings languishing in Vick's cruelty chambers.

One of our foster parents, Caroline—a retired Navy Commander—stopped by with her daughter to pick up a dog that day, and was extremely unhappy about the treatment of our organization by the state vet's office and local animal control. It was the first time she'd been to our facility, and so therefore saw everything they were seeing with fresh eyes; she was furious as a result, because she "saw only animals in good health, with plenty of water and room for exercise and obviously in good hands."

The state vet's office subsequently told the news media that we were working without approval from state, and that we'd been told earlier in the year to stop taking in dogs. The first part was true enough—only because we hadn't known in the beginning and they hadn't followed through on further steps we needed to take—but the last part was categorically false.

Sherry Helsel had given us verbal instructions of improvements desired in January when she visited; but she also told me they were here to work WITH us, not against us.

She'd "requested" the following safety measures, which were immediately carried out by the organization:

1. Created gates barring the dogs from rushing the front door.
2. Used state forms for each dog in and out of the facility, and kept very clear record of their comings and goings using spreadsheets and paper documents.
3. Posted open hours each day from 10 a.m to 2 p.m. both outside the gate and on the doors. The gates were subsequently open to the public only during those hours.
4. Finished our large fenced area in the field so that dogs could run safely and still be contained.

All these instructions were followed, implemented, and completed.

We awaited further requested modifications and/or approval, but at no point were we told we couldn't take in any new dogs. There exists no paper trail with any DDB signature stating as such, because it never happened.

PETA provided a reporter with a freedom of information request wherein they received the email from Sherry Helsel to Dan Kovich with regard to our facility. The reporter sent it along to me.

In the email, Ms. Helsel tells Dr. Kovich that she "became aware of the establishment of this facility." This is amusing, in that, as I stated before, we made no effort to hide it. We certainly had no idea we required some kind of state permission to create a home for our dogs.

She further states that, "she was unable to determine that the facility constituted a reasonable and comfortable environment for the dogs due to the noncompliant animal housing structures on the premises." By this she is talking about the sheds and Vick's kennels! She then includes a bunch of photos from inside the sheds, implying that's where our dogs lived. Please.

Helsel goes on to say, "the facility permits animals to run

at large on the grounds (heinous crime!) and uses the enclosed yard as a confinement area for exercise." (Say it ain't so! The horror!)

Her final complaint is that we hadn't filed the required paperwork (since we didn't know it was required) but had since done so. Apparently we weren't too bright, though, because, according to her, we hadn't done it correctly.

In this email to him, she says nothing about telling us we couldn't take in dogs, and she admits she hadn't been back to our facility since.

If the state was so concerned about the rightness of our facility, why did they not show up for six months the first time, and then wait another six months before showing up again?

It made zero sense.

Mind you, the state vet's office concerns itself mainly with the PHYSICAL safety of dogs . . . meaning they'd rather see them sitting solo in cages like they do in animal shelters the world over so they don't get into any kind of altercations with one another.

But DDB was not willing to keep our dogs in kennels; that was not our goal or our mission. While the state expressed horror that our dogs ran the property twice a day and were therefore subject to interaction with other dogs and critters roaming the field, I was horrified that they expected me to cage our dogs 24/7. It wouldn't happen.

Although continuous caging might keep dogs from fighting or getting injured physically, it doesn't keep them from suffering the emotional and psychological trauma that comes with that kind of confinement.

Those were the kinds of situations we were rescuing dogs FROM. It's akin to us as humans sitting in a jail cell for life versus climbing a mountain or driving a vehicle. Yes, experiencing what the world has to offer comes with risks, but I'm pretty sure every being on the planet would choose the risks over the prison cell.

Not interested in a repeat of what had happened on the county level, and with the stakes even higher now, I hired an attorney to take on the state vet's office on our behalf. After a few months of back and forth—and jumping through more hoops, such as gating off the kitchen area and ensuring that our back field stayed mowed—we finally got a Virginia state vet's office letter of approval on December 3, 2012.

COMMONWEALTH *of* VIRGINIA

Matthew J. Lohr
Commissioner

Department of Agriculture and Consumer Services
Division of Animal & Food Industry Services
Office of Animal Care and Health Policy
P.O. Box 1163, Richmond, Virginia 23218
Phone: 804/786-2483 • Fax: 804/371-2380 • Hearing Impaired: 800/828-1120
www.vdacs.virginia.gov

December 3, 2012

Dogs Deserve Better, Inc.
C/o Stallings, Bush & Randall P.C.
143 North Main Street
Suffolk, VA 23434-4507

To Dogs Deserve Better, Inc.:

On November 30, 2012 I performed a site visit to the Good Newz Rehabilitation Center operated by Dogs Deserve Better, Inc. at 1915 Moonlight Road, Smithfield, Virginia. The purpose of this visit was to determine if the facility met all laws and requirements with regard to confinement and disposition of animals, and provided a reasonable and comfortable climate appropriate to the animals housed. These conditions appeared to have been met. The facility is hereby approved by the Office of the State Veterinarian as per Section 3.2-6548 of the Code of Virginia to confine and dispose of animals. Please do not hesitate to contact me via telephone at 804-786-2483 or by email at Dan.Kovich@vdacs.virginia.gov if you have any questions regarding this approval.

Sincerely,

Daniel A. Kovich, DVM, MPH
Program Manager

This leads me to a very serious question: why didn't Vick have to get approval to chain up more than 50 dogs in his woods? I was told it's because the organization owned the property, which meant we were automatically classified as an animal shelter, thereby falling under state vet's office rules.

There appear to be NO rules for dog fighters and dog breeders and hunters in the state of Virginia. While I'm not on board with the way we were treated by the state vet's office, I do agree there should be oversight of shelters and rescues.

That oversight, however, should consist of guidance and help, as opposed to condemnation, especially in initial stages with organizations who are willing to comply with reasonable requests, but don't know or understand what is expected of them.

There are many horror stories of rescues and shelters gone wrong out there, and if having some kind of oversight prevents those kinds of situations, I'm all for it.

Yet exempting people like Michael Vick and the dog breeders, dogfighters, and hunters, too, is unacceptable. Most of the animal cruelty taking place in the state of Virginia—and across the country—isn't happening in rescues or shelters. It's happening in backyards and the unregulated industries that are rampant with abuse and neglect.

Marley loved nothing more than chasing her ball. Photo by Rita Thomas.

Jada looked gorgeous. It didn't matter. They seized her anyway.

CHAPTER THIRTY-FOUR:
Arrested. For Animal Cruelty?

Imagine you have guns in your house, like many Americans. This isn't illegal, and you want to protect yourself and your family against a worst-case scenario situation such as a zombie apocalypse or, more boringly, a standard home invasion.

You have gun safes in a few areas of the house, just in case . . . you feel strongly you need to be able to reach protective measures in an emergency situation.

But the neighbors want your property, because they've found out there's "gold in them thar hills"; it's situated directly under your house, in fact.

These folks obviously can't get to that prize—the gold—unless they get rid of you. They know you have guns, so armed with this smidgen of truth, they call the police and report that you've shot and killed your whole family.

Except direct evidence doesn't support the claims. When the police break down your door, your family is alive and well, sitting in the living room with you as you all laugh and watch a movie together. You're drinking sodas and eating popcorn when the door blows off its hinges.

Not only are you terrified, you're downright flummoxed as to why they've even barged into your home.

Did they get the wrong house?

Instead of the police shrugging their shoulders, apologizing about your door and the bad info, and reporting to your accusers that there is obviously nothing wrong—perhaps even warning them that filing false reports is a crime—*the police arrest you anyway.*

Because someone told them you killed your family. And if someone said it, it must be true—even though all discernible facts attest to the opposite.

The police seize all your guns, refuse to tell you what you've done wrong, and tell the media that you were shooting your family—daily. You look around at your wife or husband and kids in confusion. Not one of your family members has a single bullet wound. Or bruises. Or any signs that they've been harmed in any way, by you or anyone else.

Would you conclude that the police were corrupt?

Could they be conspiring for their portion of the gold?

It would be hard to conclude otherwise.

I got back to the center at noon on August 27th—after ten days away—and was arrested by 4:00 p.m. for animal cruelty.

I had no idea what was happening to me or why.

Our facility had been fully staffed while I was gone, and no dogs were harmed or left unattended. An employee had overnighted each night, too, just in case.

Surry County, or one of their co-conspirators, had called the media to alert them that I was being arrested.

In fact, everyone knew about it before I did.

There were helicopters flying overhead and media vans in our driveway.

ACO Tracy Terry brought along the sheriff and two deputies for maximum intimidation.

Animal Control Officer Tracy Terry, a white female who I'd never met before, looked at me with eyes of hatred. She brought the sheriff and at least two deputies with her; when I asked why I being arrested, she said "Ask your attorney."

At the time, I didn't even have an attorney.

I instructed dog caretaker Corrie L. to grab the camera and take photos of everything that went on. I'm incredibly grateful I had the presence of mind to do so, because I shudder to think what may have happened if we hadn't. I was used to documenting everything when I worked chained dog cases, so it was second nature to me to make sure we had a visual record.

If it was my word against Tracy Terry's, I didn't even have to ask which of us would get the benefit of the doubt.

Unfortunately, Corrie was nervous and stressed, and put the camera on the wrong setting; as a result, many of the photos came out blurry. However, we got enough to catalog for our supporters the reality of the intimidation used against me and the organization.

Corrie initially began filming the interactions, but was threatened by the sheriff that if she didn't stop he would seize our camera. We had every legal right to videotape their activities on our property, but Corrie switched to photos instead, just in case.

Jada stares at Tracy Terry. I think there was someone she didn't like, but it wasn't me.

Tracy Terry informed me she was seizing one of our dogs, a pitbull named Jada—even though the dog wasn't injured and hadn't been harmed in any way. On the contrary, our girl looked simply amazing compared to the beat up, skinny, sickly pup she'd been when she first arrived at our facility the previous November.

Jada was now sleek, muscular, and healthy, beloved by staff and volunteers alike.

What right had they to take her?

Tracy Terry had also neglected to list Jada on the search warrant, making her seizure illegal.

I held it together while they were onsite, not wanting to give them the satisfaction of seeing me fall apart. I was extremely unnerved and perplexed by the officer's apparent hatred for me. I never met her, had never seen her, knew nothing about her. What was happening that would allow her to treat a complete stranger like this?

I felt I'd landed in an alternate reality, and not a pleasant one.

Jada and I sit quietly together while the deputy with a belt full of weapons books me.

Jada and I sat next to each other; she on the kuranda bed chewing on her toy—completely unaware she was about to be taken—and me sitting sadly beside her, unable to protect her, unable to protect either of us.

It's obvious from the photo that Jada's not afraid of me. A dog who's being harmed by someone will either cower from that person or show aggression toward them. Jada simply accepted me as part of her pack and went about her business.

Tracy Terry, the sheriff, and his deputies were in our facility for about an hour, seizing all our Halt pepper spray and the smaller of our two stun guns, which the officer had called a "taser" on the search warrant.

I guess we weren't allowed anything to protect ourselves from attack by humans or animals. Ironically, animal control officer Tracy Terry carried a gun, a taser, a billy club, and pepper spray.

We were entitled to nothing.

When they finally left, taking Jada with them, I spoke to a

lawyer I'd met recently during our Chain Off event in Richmond, Virginia. We'd talked about working together to pass better laws for the dogs, yet now I was humiliated and ashamed that I instead had to call him for a much grimmer reason, a storyline wherein I was being portrayed as the bad guy.

He advised me not to speak to the press, who still lingered outside, hoping to get some juicy footage for their nightly stories.

SEARCH WARRANT
Commonwealth of Virginia   VA. CODE §§ 19.2-56, 19.2-57

TO ANY AUTHORIZED OFFICER:
　　　You are hereby commanded in the name of the Commonwealth to forthwith search the following place, person or thing either in day or night
Two story house with attached garage as well as the curtilage located at 1915 Moonlight Road, Smithfield, VA 23430.

　for the following property, objects and/or persons:
Any and all paperwork in relationship to past and present animals that were/are housed on premises. All receipts for mace or tasers bought by Dogs Deserve Better. All Veterinarian paperwork to include but not limited to all bills and visits of all animals that were/are housed on property. Tasers and mace used on the animals as well as anything used as cruel treatment on the animals.

You are further commanded to seize said property, persons, and/or objects if they be found and to produce before the _____Surry_____ Circuit Court an inventory of all property, persons, and/or objects seized.

This SEARCH WARRANT is issued in relation to an offense substantially described as follows:
3.2-6570; 3.2-6503

Jada was never listed on a search warrant. Without being at death's door, her seizure was illegal.

I had nothing to hide in our facility; in fact, it was the exact opposite. I felt pride in what we'd accomplished on a shoestring budget, and I WANTED them to showcase how beautiful and well-cared-for our dogs and property were. I needed them to run footage of happy dogs and clean floors, to wedge at least some doubt into the minds of the discerning public.

Decision made, I instructed staff to allow the media into the home and dog yards and let them see every single dog and every single fenced area or room. Nothing was to be off limits to them.

We had nothing to hide—except me.

I stayed in my room, as per attorney instructions.

I couldn't bear to watch the news stories about that horrific day because it was just too painful. One of our supporters from Pennsylvania sent me the following email right after seeing it on her local news station.

"Tonight's WTAJ report featured videos of your home and the surroundings—believe it or not, the most absurd contradiction I've ever seen: the damaging oral report went on and on, while scenes of healthy, obviously happy and contented dogs ambled freely through a spotless interior—and outside, dogs were free in fenced enclosures."

That night, I paced my room, alone; if I'd ever had a dark night of the soul, this was it. I was terrified, angry, and bereft, crying for hours. I wanted to die and leave this horror show behind, but I was too much of a coward to off myself, and I didn't want to do that to my children, Joe, or my mother. There were a few people who I actually mattered to in this world, and I couldn't abandon them to feel the pain and anger of my loss.

Besides, I knew doing myself in would just make me look guilty in the eyes of the world; no matter what they said, that was one thing I wasn't.

I felt intense shame, but not because I'd committed a crime; rather because I'd been very publicly and falsely accused, and humiliated in the worst way possible for an animal rescuer.

That day, I lost everything.

My reputation, any feeling of safety in my world, and what little self-confidence remained had all been stripped from me. I felt violated, exposed. I would never again feel secure knowing how easily an innocent person can be arrested and maligned, with no recourse and no way to stop the injustice.

My mind raced, going over and over what'd happened, trying to figure out the hows and whys of it all. I hadn't yet understood the part Deana played in all of this, and I couldn't piece together how Surry County could possibly arrest me. Had they falsified evidence? If so, what was it?

The richest irony was that I spent so much of my time trying to get real abusers charged for killing or harming dogs, and I always failed. In some cases, there would be reams of evidence, a dead or dying dog, and yet nothing I did succeeded in getting any of the abusers I dealt with charged.

Ezekiel after surgery to clean up and stitch his wounds. He'd been very lucky.

Oh, there was that one time . . .

A German shepherd had been dumped along the road near a church in Pennsylvania, and was starving, seeking out nearby humans for help. Someone shot him, but succeeded only in wounding the poor guy, the bullet going through the back of his ear and tracking up the side of his forehead. An inch to the left would have been enough to kill him.

While Christmas should have been the season of compassion, it seemed the parishioners of Joan of Arc Catholic Church in Frugality, Pennsylvania, missed the memo that year. Sources told us not only did the priest ask the congregation to "get rid of the dog" who'd started hanging around, but parishioners were reportedly saying things like "don't go over to the left of the church, there's a shepherd lurking over there."

Seems no one offered the dog aid or food, and certainly not

a home or a warm bed. Yet he lingered, making a den in the corner of the church building under a bush; tired, thirsty, hungry, and cold. He had nowhere else to go.

I named the shepherd Ezekiel since he was saved outside a church, for it says in Ezekiel 3:8-9: "Behold, I have made thy face strong against their faces, and thy forehead strong against their foreheads. As an adamant harder than flint have I made thy forehead: fear them not, neither be dismayed at their looks, though they be a rebellious house."

I believe that a higher power was looking after Ezekiel, and I believe that members of the church were given a spiritual test and failed. Instead of taking in God's creature in desperate need of human kindness, they shunned him, ignored him, and even tried to kill him.

The day we went to rescue the dog (and unbeknownst to us at the time), his shooter pulled up behind our van with some cohorts to finish the job; our presence there foiled their efforts. There has never been a doubt in my mind that an angel protected Ezekiel that day. It's a shame that dogs even need divine intervention . . . shouldn't we humans have enough compassion in our souls to care for them ourselves?

The case made the local news, and finally a suspect, Jason Hockenberry, confessed and pleaded guilty, claiming "he was protecting himself from a loose, potentially violent dog."

At Hockenberry's sentencing hearing, I was honored to stand and read a statement on behalf of Ezekiel, to voice the very real fear the dog had to have undergone, to have the plight of an animal taken seriously in a court of law. The experience was unforgettable.

It would be the only time in my 13 years of fighting for dogs that I succeeded in having someone charged with cruelty.[*]

---

[*] Watch Ezekiel's story at https://bit.ly/34kdBYw

Jada upon arrival
at our facility,
November 6, 2011

Jada was beat up, with wounds on her face, rear, and thighs when she came to us.

CHAPTER THIRTY-FIVE:

A Volunteer's Love for our Center, Jada, and Woody

All of our rescued dogs were special, but Jada easily won the heart of one of our earliest volunteers, Melanie Gilbert. She put it this way:

I came to Dogs Deserve Better as a visitor in 2011 at the invitation of my good friend and long-time DDB volunteer, Leslie. I'd been going through a rough divorce, and had lost both of my dogs to my ex-husband.

Leslie suggested I go to the Center to get "doggie therapy." I was nervous. As a life-long lover of animals, I knew what most "rescue" centers looked like: sad dogs that had been abused and abandoned, waiting behind the bars of cages for months at a time, hoping for a new family. I wasn't sure if I could emotionally handle seeing that.

Leslie assured me this place was very different from any other rescue or adoption center I'd ever visited. On that promise I agreed to travel the hour or so distance the following weekend. I was not disappointed. The center was open, clean, vibrant, and alive with happy, wagging tails.

I was delighted to learn that each dog was walked twice daily. The veterinarian care was second to none. They enlisted professional trainers and touch therapists to help with rehabilitation. The dogs were not behind bars, but separated into amicable groups for socialization and playtime. The only time they spent in their individual crates (complete with padding and blankets) was during the designated afternoon nap times, for breakfast and dinner, and at bedtime.

I met Tami on that first trip out to DDB, and immediately recognized her as a kindred soul. She quickly became (and remains) a friend, confidante, and personal hero. I met, and fell in love with, many dogs during the time I volunteered for Dogs Deserve Better. There will forever be two dogs that will hold a special place in my heart: Jada and Woody.

Jada had been brought to the center very young and covered with what appeared to be road rash. I spent many an hour with Jada playing, grooming, and cuddling her. Jada was sweet, playful, and always seemed to know when you just needed someone to sit quietly by your side. I credit her for helping me heal from the emotional wounds inflicted by my divorce.

By the summer of 2012 I was experiencing yet another life trauma. My mother had been diagnosed with Stage 4 colon cancer, and I'd been her caretaker for more than a year. She was approaching the end of her life, and I had to make the decision to transfer her to a nursing home. This was incredibly painful, and my time spent at Dogs Deserve Better once again became therapeutic.

That was the summer I met Woody. He'd been rescued from

a terrible situation in Indiana and adopted by a family in New York. He was a little more "special needs" than the family was able to provide for, so he was brought to The Good Newz Rehab Center in Virginia. I was there the morning he arrived, and he seemed to echo my exact emotions . . . tired, unsure of the future, and not very trusting of anyone's intentions.

He seemed to have a look on his face that said "If one more stressful thing happens to me, I just won't be able to bear it!" I knew that look entirely too well, as I had seen it on my own face countless times over the past two years. By and by I made Woody my foster dog, then several months later I decided to complete the adoption paperwork on him. He'd become my four-legged soul mate.

Melanie snuggles with Woody as he slowly learns to trust again.

Woody taught me about resiliency and the ability to bounce back from a bad situation. He taught me how to love and trust again, and what real friendship and support looks like. Five years later, when he crossed the bridge, he taught me that love continues on outside of our physical plane.

My volunteer time at Dogs Deserve Better ended in 2013 when I moved out of state, but the lessons, memories, and friendships I made while there continue on even today. I will be forever grateful I had the opportunity to work with such an amazing organization.　　　　　　　　　　　　　　*—Melanie Gilbert*

Surry County
Pound - Feces,
No Food, No
Water, Taken
August 31, 2012
1:00 p.m.

The Surry County Animal Shelter, where they'd supposedly taken Jada. It was disgusting.

CHAPTER THIRTY-SIX:
Worried for Jada, and Myself

What had they done with our girl?
We were seriously concerned for Jada's welfare.
I'm told the news ran video of them putting her into the animal

control vehicle, and she looked beautiful . . . not at all like the dogs one would normally see being seized for neglect.

Even though the media was, knowingly or not, enabling Surry County's smear campaign, they were still running the footage of beautiful dogs with every story. It was enough to make folks with a few brain cells in their heads question the legitimacy of the arrest.

I'd done the right thing by letting them in to see all the dogs and every area of our facility.

It was a well-documented fact that Surry County common-wealth attorney Gerald Poindexter had thwarted the arrest of Michael Vick for animal cruelty and dogfighting.

That's why the feds had to come in and do it themselves.

Poindexter was also furious with the animal rights groups who were relentless in their pursuit of justice against Michael Vick.

What better way for him to get revenge than by taking down the naïve (i.e. idiotic) animal rights activist who dared buy Vick's property for the very same crime?

The plan was beautiful in its ugliness.

In addition to my worry for Jada, I was worried about my own mental state; I was struggling to keep up a brave front for the staff, dogs, and volunteers at the center, and I had nowhere to go to feel safe, nowhere to go to fall apart.

I put myself in counseling at a center in Williamsburg, Virginia, and took the ferry 1-2 times a week just to be somewhere I was allowed to talk, allowed to cry, allowed to be broken.

In my first session I barely spoke; I couldn't, due to the sobs that wrenched themselves free of the chains binding my soul together.

Therapy, aka crying, helped, at least a little.

It was all I had.

Jada had ostensibly been taken to the Surry County Animal Shelter. We hadn't heard good things about the place, and it made us very nervous. In fact, when Vick's dogs were seized, two of them "disappeared" from the Surry shelter, never to be seen again.

Even though no evidence ever came to light as proof of what happened to those dogs, it was commonly "understood" that corrupt officials in Surry County conspired to send them wherever Vick wanted them to go.

They just "poofed" into thin air.

The day after Jada was taken, our staff member Corrie and a volunteer drove to the Surry County Animal Shelter during their open hours to do a welfare check on our dog. Jada wasn't there, and animal control officer Tracy Terry tried to keep them out, even though she had no legal right to do so.

Why?

Where was our dog?

Conditions at the shelter were awful, and Corrie took photos of it; it was laughable that a place that looked as bad as theirs had the nerve to seize a dog from another organization. Each of the kennels sported multiple piles of feces, and there was not a speck of visible food or water.

At 1:00 in the afternoon?

Jada looked worried when she was about to be seized, but she was still healthy, beautiful.

Jada gives Tracy Terry the hairy eyeball. She's obviously unafraid of me.

CHAPTER THIRTY-SEVEN:
A Hearing for Jada

"I ASKED HOW VICK GOT AWAY WITH IT. REX LAUGHED AND SHRUGGED HIS SHOULDERS. I TOOK THIS TO MEAN THAT IF VICK WAS FIGHTING DOGS, HE MUST KNOW HE HAD NOTHING TO FEAR FROM LOCAL AUTHORITIES."
—KATHY STROUSE, "BADD NEWZ: THE UNTOLD STORY OF THE MICHAEL VICK DOG FIGHTING CASE"

Virginia law states that when animal control seizes a dog, a hearing on the dog's custody MUST take place within 10 days. No ifs, ands, or buts about it.

Yet a little thing like the law didn't stop Surry County civil attorney Mr. Hefty from proposing to my attorney, Mr. Jones, that we make a "winner takes all" agreement with regards to Jada. In effect, we would put off her hearing until my trial took place, and if I won I could have the dog back.

My response? "Absolutely not."

I'd been to court multiple times by now, and I knew how the court system worked. Continuances—for multiple reasons—are more normal than not, and it could be a year before my case actually went to trial. There was no way I was allowing them to hold onto Jada for even a minute longer than the ten days the law granted them.

All our staff and volunteers were upset at her loss, and we all worried for her constantly. Was she ok? Would she disappear too?

We all pondered the same question: why did they choose Jada to seize out of all the dogs? If I were supposedly cruel, why wouldn't they seize all of them?

Jada had been a favorite of Deana and Andrea, and by this point I was starting to put two and two together. Had they singled her out? And if so, why?

Another in a long line of oddities, i.e. illegalities, about the Surry County court system was that I never received written notice of our hearing date. My attorney had to call and find out when we were to be there.

This is an incredibly blatant violation of the rights of the accused. Not one time did I receive a single notice with a court date or other information from the Surry County court system. How was Surry County, Virginia's "justice system" allowed to operate so far outside the rules?

On the day of our hearing for Jada, I took seven witnesses— three volunteers, our dog caretakers, Melissa the new office manager, and mobile vet Dr. Dragon—as well as our attorney, Robert Jones from the nearby town of Smithfield.

Oddly, animal control officer Tracy Terry had no witnesses, aside from herself.

That fact alone gave me reason to experience an odd feeling: hope.

Deana's patsy, former dog caretaker Andrea Wheeler, had failed to show up.

The next chapter provides a transcript of the hearing, in full. Note that Tracy Terry's testimony has no substance to it, and she can't get her dates straight—ever.

The officer first showed up at our facility July 20, 2012, while Joe and I were vacationing in Florida. She then showed up again, accompanied by the state vet's office, on August 23, 2012, when I was in St. Lucia.

She came back August 27, 2012 to arrest me for cruelty.

There, I did her job for her.

Jada as her initial injuries are healing up, running in the field.

No bones about it, I was terrified to go into court that day. I'd already been arrested and stood trial for Doogie in Pennsylvania, but in that case I freely admitted to taking the dog. It was the "why" I took the dog that mattered, and the "why" was to save a life. There's no better reason, in my opinion, and I wore the consequences I received for my actions as a badge of honor.

I'd also gotten a citation for trespassing for helping other dogs chained on an abandoned piece of property; once again, their lives were well worth it, and many of those dogs gained their freedom as a result.

In this case, the charges were false, and I was painted as a monster.

It felt completely different, and really, really bad.

Was the judge corrupt, too?

Was he or she in their pocket?

I didn't know.

And what I didn't know terrified me.

I'd obsessed about what I could have done to deserve this, but I couldn't remember any time that I'd been anything approaching cruel with the animals. Not only that, but in that month between July 20th and August 23rd, I'd only acted as caretaker maybe 2 or 3 days, other than the days I trained new caretakers Corrie and Nick.

I'd been hiring more help, and getting back to my own front lines activist work of fighting for the rights of chained dogs.

Unless their implication was that I had instructed staff to harm the dogs, I couldn't see what kind of evidence they could possibly have.

Worst case scenario, I had to be prepared for the possibility that they had photoshopped or doctored evidence somehow. It was the only thing that made sense to me. *Why and who would go to court with zero evidence?*

How good would their doctored evidence be?

I nervously awaited the answers to these questions.

Jada upon arrival at our facility, November 6, 2011

Another of Jada's "before" photos. A large wound up by her tail.

CHAPTER THIRTY-EIGHT:

We Want Jada Back
September 11, 2012

"YEAH FINE. I KILLED THE DOGS. I HUNG THEM. I SLAMMED THEM. I KILLED ALL OF THEM. I LOST F@*KING MILLIONS, ALL OVER SOME F@*KING DOGS."—MICHAEL VICK, OCTOBER 12, 2007, AFTER FAILING HIS POLYGRAPH

Gerald Poindexter charged Vick with cruelty and dogfighting only AFTER the feds charged him, because they'd made him look bad. He later dismissed the animal cruelty charges and declared a "time served" on the fighting charges.

VIRGINIA, IN THE GENERAL DISTRICT COURT
OF THE COUNTY OF SURRY:

COMMONWEALTH
v.
TAMIRA THAYNE

AS HEARD BEFORE THE HONORABLE
BRUCE CLARK

SEPTEMBER 11, 2012

PRESENT: Mr. William Hefty, On behalf of the Commonwealth
Mr. Robert W. Jones, Jr., On behalf of the Defendant

THE COURT: What we have today is the 10-day requirement on this situation. So everybody is ready to hear this today; is that correct?

MR. HEFTY: Your Honor, we would ask for a one-week continuance. We have a witness who's material that's in North Carolina. Because of the statutory 10 days, she could not be here. It requires a hearing, it doesn't require you to make a decision within the 10 days, so we'd like a one-week continuance.

MR. JONES: We object to that continuance, Judge. We have a number of people here who have taken off work to be here as witnesses. The statute says 10 days.

THE COURT: The problem I guess I have, the statute—to say I have a hearing without a decision, but—says I can make a delayed decision but I have to hear evidence, but I think unless— you have to point out to me—I think the statute says it has to be done in 10 days.

MR. HEFTY: I mean I could have part of a hearing today, at the end of the hearing I'd ask for a continuance of a week to finish the hearing.

I don't know that the hearing has to be completed in 10 days.

THE COURT: Has to be started within 10 days; we all say good morning and continue it?

MR. HEFTY: It just makes more sense to jointly continue it for a week, ask for a continuance after half of the hearing, but the 10-day requirement makes it hard to get a witness here who's out of state who's material, and so—

THE COURT: And unfortunately you certainly didn't—I presume you didn't write the statute. I certainly didn't. Mr. Jones didn't.

And I understand the statute has good meanings and purposes. But sometimes these quick-response things do run into problems with the practical approach on them. But—it's difficult. Let me look at it, but I don't—see how mandatory this looks. We'll take it from that approach here.

The problem I'm looking at is that the hearing shall be not—shall not be, but it just keeps us on our toes—shall be not more than 10 business days from the date of the seizure of the animal. And if it "can be" for a good cause shown or any other out I would love to do it, but this is pretty "shall be." The hearing. And I think when the—I mean the hearing, I think as we all know what a hearing is, it's put the evidence on and reach the conclusion.

Certainly things can be deferred. I'm afraid I'm—over the objection of Mr. Jones, I'm afraid the statute says we got to have it in 10 days. I think the reason for it is you seized an animal. You know, we don't want to seize it and deny the person the right to the animal. The fact the seizure was not founded, certainly not saying that. So I am afraid, you know, that doesn't—that doesn't mean that another petition can't be taken out at another time, you understand that, if your case doesn't go well. I'm not saying it's not going to go well. If you can show me some language that says I've got any room on the 10 days I'd love to do it, because I'd rather hear a full, fair hearing, but I don't see the—I don't see the evidence here.

MR. POINDEXTER: Well, Judge, if I may speak on behalf of the County.

THE COURT: Certainly.

MR. POINDEXTER: They are here. The parties are here.

Notice was given, the parties are here. But I see—I wouldn't imagine there's any reason why the Court could not grant a continuance if it felt it would be the expedient thing to do to get rid of the case. I mean, they're here, and that's the most important thing. And you can do virtually anything you want to do once they're present.

[Note, the hearing for the return of Jada was a civil proceeding, NOT a criminal hearing. This is why Mr. Hefty was the commonwealth attorney for the matter, NOT Poindexter. It is telling that Poindexter came and insinuated himself into the hearing anyway, trying to get a continuance.]

THE COURT: Well, yeah, but I don't—I just have a problem with the language. There's no other crime that I'm aware of. I mean there may be others that says a hearing shall be had within X days. You know, and I agree, if I heard the evidence and wanted to think about it, I think I can do that. But I think I've got to have the hearing within 10 days. I think it might be a good thing to recommend to the General Assembly to give us an out that says for good cause shown, but I just don't see it. I just—I don't know how to get around that. I would much rather hear a case always on the merits. Always on the merits if possible. But I think the General Assembly said I don't have that option. So if I don't have the option—I may be wrong. And you know, I don't think whatever we do today is res judicata.

I mean I think if things go—don't go the right way, and the conditions exist, you can always take another petition. That would be my ruling. But I think we've got to have this today absent the—absent the consent of the defendant. So having said that, I overrule your motion, and we need to proceed.

Ms. Thayne, Mr. Jones, today all we're hearing is the petition. So it's a particular section of the Virginia Code that asks—they've seized a dog and basically they're asking that the dog be disposed of because the dog has been treated cruelly or is in bad condition.

MR. POINDEXTER: If Your Honor please—

THE COURT: So you understand that, and you're ready to go? Mr. Jones you're ready to go?

MR. JONES: Yes, sir.

THE COURT: I'm going to put these two aside because they're not really before us. We're here on a petition.

All right, all persons that will testify in this matter, please raise your right hand.

(The witnesses were duly sworn.)

THE COURT: All right, thank you. And Mr. Hefty—

MR. HEFTY: Tracy Terry.

Tracy Terry—Direct

TRACY TERRY, having been duly sworn, was called as a witness on behalf of the Commonwealth, and testified as follows:

DIRECT EXAMINATION
BY MR. HEFTY:

Q: Will you state your position?

A: I'm Chief Animal Control Officer for Surry County.

Q: And did you have a search warrant to go to 1915 Moonlight Road to investigate alleged animal abuse?

A: Yes.

Q: And what day did you do that?

A: The original date I went to investigate was August the 27th.

Q: And did you seize a dog on that day?

A: No.

Q: What day did you seize the dog?

A: I seized the dog on—I'm sorry. Yes, I did. I seized—I originally went out on September the 24th and did seize the dog on September the 27th.

THE COURT: August. August 24th.

A: I'm sorry, August. Yes.

Q: You seized the dog on August 27th?

A: Yes.

Q: And could you describe the dog that you seized?

A: It was a female black and white pit bull, approximately one years old, approximately 60, 70 pounds.

Q: And can you tell the Court why you thought the dog was cruelly treated or hadn't been provided adequate care?

A: I know the dog was being crated up to 20 hours a day.

MR. JONES: Judge, I would ask her to tell us how she would know a dog is crated 20 hours a day upon her observation.

THE WITNESS: Um—

THE COURT: All right, there's an objection to the admissibility of the evidence.

BY MR. HEFTY:

Q: Was there any way that—let me rephrase the question. Was there any way that you knew that the dog was crated 20 hours a day by your observations?

A: No.

Q: Okay. How else did you know that the dog was cruelly treated or hadn't been provided adequate care?

A: I had received several complaints not on just this dog individual, but on several that they weren't receiving veterinary care—

MR. JONES: Judge, I will object for the purpose of her knowing that. For the purpose for investigation it's fine.

THE COURT: Truth of the matter is out; because of complaints she took certain actions is in.

MR. JONES: Right.

BY MR. HEFTY:

Q: By observing the dog, what did you see that was evidence of denial of adequate care?

A: Um, the—I have pictures that were sent to me, and I—on—during the day of the search warrant I took all vet records and records pertaining to this pit bull, and there was no veterinarian care for this animal in regards to this attack she was in.

[Note: She was not in any attack, hence there couldn't possibly be vet records for a nonexistent incident. She participated in the attack on Anthony in April, but she was never attacked by another dog. And she had no marks on her.]

MR. JONES: Judge, again, if it's for the purpose of the truth of the matter, she's saying an attack she was in.

THE COURT: You might have her explain that a little bit if you can.

BY MR. HEFTY:

Q: Can you explain what you saw on the dog that was evidence of attack?

A: I previously went out there on July the 27th and saw this dog. There were scars and marks on the dog that were not there when I went out on the 20—on July 20th that were there then on August the 24th.

Q: And can you describe how recent those were, whether they were bloody, what they looked like?

A: No, they were healed over.

Q: And could you tell—

THE COURT: What date are we talking about that they were healed over?

THE WITNESS: When I went there on the 24th.

THE COURT: Of August.

THE WITNESS: Right.

THE COURT: All right, go ahead.

BY MR. HEFTY:

Q: And could you tell what caused those marks?

A: It appeared to me to be an attack from another dog.

Q: And could you tell whether veterinarian care had been provided for those?

A: In accordance to their own records, it hasn't.

Q: Could you tell that by looking at the dog?

A: No.

Q: Okay. And did you find evidence of mace at the—

A: Yes. On both occasions that I visited, there was mace displayed all throughout the house. One on the kitchen island, one on the office manager's desk, one in the bathroom located where the pit bull was crated. And that was on both occasions. When I went back out on the 27th, it was all put in a closet and drawers and everything else. There was none visually on site when I went and did the search warrant.

Q: Okay. And could you tell that mace had been used on this particular dog?

A: I mean to say a hundred percent myself, no, I can't. The dog did have bloodshot eyes, tearing of the eyes, but to say that I, you know, can tell that the dog had been maced, no. Of course that's where my witness comes in, and she's not here.

Q: Okay. Was there anything else from your observation that you could tell the Court about that the dog was—had been mistreated, or had not been provided adequate care?

A: Unh-uh.

MR. HEFTY: That's all I have, Your Honor.

CROSS-EXAMINATION
BY MR. JONES:

Q: Is this the dog in question? (Showing photographs.)

A: Um-hmm. Yes.

Q: Does that, to your knowledge, represent what it looked like the day you came and seized it?

A: Yes.

Q: (Showed witness additional photographs.)

A: Yes. Um-hmm.

THE COURT: You've seen these, no objection?

MR. HEFTY: I haven't, but no objection.

THE COURT: All right, thank you.

BY MR. JONES:

Q: And the mace you speak of, that was actually Halt!, a pepper spray that's used by postmen and things of that nature?

A: Yes.

Q: Not, mace, Halt!, h-a-l-t.

THE COURT: Used by who?

MR. JONES: Postmen.

I don't believe I have any other questions.

MR. HEFTY: Object to the comment about a postman.

[Note: I'm sorry, but that's just darn funny. "Object to the comment about a postman."]

THE COURT: All right.

MR. JONES: But it is a product made for dog repellent.

THE WITNESS: Right. But it is not made to be constantly used on an animal.

THE COURT: All right. Any other evidence?

MR. HEFTY: No.

MR. JONES: Judge, I'd move to strike at this point. The evidence is there was this Halt! in the home, and you can see the pictures of the dog.

THE COURT: Court overrules at this time. Like most first evidence, it's favorable to the Commonwealth. I understand there was some scarring and so forth, so I'll overrule at this time. Put your case on.

MR. JONES: I call my client first.

TAMIRA THAYNE, having been duly sworn, was called as a witness in her own behalf, and testified as follows:

DIRECT EXAMINATION
BY MR. JONES:

Q: You are Ms. Thayne?

A: Yes. *[Unfortunately. Ha!]*

Q: And what is your role or title there?

A: I'm the founder and CEO of Dogs Deserve Better. We're a nonprofit organization—

REPORTER: Excuse me. Could you speak up a little bit?

A: Yes. My name is Tamira Thayne. I'm the founder and CEO of Dogs Deserve Better. It's a nonprofit organization that works solely for chained and penned dogs, to bring them into the home and family.

Q: And the dog in question, the animal that was seized, the dog was named Jada?

A: Yes.

Q: And when did your —when did you-all come into possession of her?

A: We got Jada November 6th, I believe, of 2011. From the best—the pictures that we have show that she had wounds when we got her.

Q: We'll get to that in a minute.

A: She was—we believe she was thrown from a moving vehicle. One of our volunteers found her along the side of the road.

Q: And that was in November of 2011?

A: Yes, November 6th of 2011.

Q: And did she receive any type of veterinary care?

A: Yes. Yes, the volunteer actually took her to the vet before bringing her to us, and then she went to the vet when she was with us for skin rashes.

She went—she was spayed at the snip van, and we have all her vet records with us.

Q: And do you have a specific veterinarian that you use, or do you use—

A: We have different veterinarians in the area. One of our veterinarians is here that we use.

She has been to our facility multiple times already.

Jada went to Ivor Veterinarian for skin rash, and she was spayed with a snip van.

THE COURT: She was what?

THE WITNESS: Spayed with a PETA snip van.

THE COURT: All right.

BY MR. JONES:

Q: The allegations that have been presented today are that on I believe it was July 20th, Ms. Terry did not observe any marks on the animal, but when she came back on August 24th there were some healed cuts or something of that nature. How many animals were in the facility during that roughly month period?

A: I think we averaged around 10 to 12.

Q: And how are the dogs kept as far as crates and pens?

A: Every dog in the facility gets two walks a day in our field. Sometimes they can run free, sometimes they are leashed, depending on the dog.

Q: Is that because of the temperament of the dog that you're talking about, based upon the dog?

A: It depends on if they want to hunt a lot in the weeds, because we want to make sure that they are safe. So they—they run twice a day in the field, and they spend a lot of time either in different areas of the house. We have two doggie doors where they can go in and out to fenced yards. We have three different fenced yards, and many different areas they can be in. So the dogs do sleep in crates, and they have nap time in crates, most dogs do, from 2 to 4 every day.

Q: The dogs that are brought to your facility, are they, for lack of better terms, abused animals when you receive them?

A: Yes. Almost always.

Q: Are they aggressive?

A: Um, typically not to people. Sometimes we have some dog issues. They don't like certain dogs. Jada didn't like female dogs. She ended up having to be just with a male dog all the time. So in the past two months she's been just mostly with a male dog.

Q: And when you say she didn't like female dogs, would they get into a territorial—

A: They would get into scuffles. Yeah, they would scuffle. She never was in a serious dog fight.

Q: And if the dog is in a minor scuffle, and gets nipped or—how are they treated from a medical standpoint?

A: We have peroxide on site. We have a lot of these cloths soaked in cleaning material that we use. So each dog is evaluated. Typically a scuffle they don't really get injured seriously enough to go to a vet. And we always monitor the situation, and if they need to go to a vet they do.

Q: If there was sign of infection or non healing, would that be what would take them to a vet, or—

A: Yes. Um-hmm.

Q: Did that happen during the month between July 20th to August 24th with Jada?

A: No, Jada was only with Hef during that entire time. Maybe Bandit.

Q: Go back. (Showing photographs to witness.)

A: Yes, those are the pictures of Jada when she arrived at our facility.

Q: And that would have been November—

A: November 6, 2011.

MR. HEFTY: No objection.

Q: The animal control officer, Ms. Terry, indicated she found mace in the home, but the Halt! pepper spray or dog repellent, you acknowledge that was in the—

A: Yes, that was provided for the safety of our staff, for their own protection and as a last case need for dogs if they had a confrontation.

Q: So is that something that is done often?

A: No. Very seldom.

THE COURT: Mr. Jones, you're moving to admit these, and you've seen them, no objection?

MR. JONES: Yes, sir.

MR. HEFTY: (Shakes head.)

BY MR. JONES:

Q: And you would like to have Jada back and—

A: Yes. Our dogs are treated wonderfully at our facility. She has a lot of love. We have great staff who takes care of her every day, and we have volunteers who come in and spend time with the dogs, and I don't feel that it's right that they could seize her based on the testimony.

MR. JONES: I don't believe I have any more questions for Ms. Thayne.

CROSS-EXAMINATION
BY MR. HEFTY:

Q: The dogs were kept in crates; is that correct?

A: They slept in crates. Most of the dogs sleep in a crate from 9:30 at night until 8 in the morning, and they nap in a crate from 2 to 4. The rest of the day we strive very hard to of have them in different areas all day so that they are not crated.

Q: Is it true that Jada was kept in a crate more than the other dogs?

A: No, that is not true.

Q: So how many hours a day was Jada kept in a crate?

A: Typically, as long as the weather was good and she had

places to be out, it was 12 and-a-half.

Q: So she was never kept in a crate for 20 hours?

A: She should have never been in a crate for 20 hours. She would have never been when I was taking care of her. If somebody else was when I wasn't there—I'm the one being charged. When I was there Jada was never kept in a crate for 20 hours a day.

Q: But you don't know whether she actually was kept in a crate for 20 hours a day.

A: I don't believe she was. No, I don't believe she was.

Q: And was Jada sprayed with the Halt!?

A: I don't believe she ever was. I don't know. I never sprayed her.

Q: Okay. And how many other people were working?

A: We had two dog caretakers. One went to another local job. One just moved to Florida. Now we have three more caretakers there.

Q: And when you weren't there you don't know whether she was sprayed with Halt!?

A: Well, no, but I don't think so.

MR. HEFTY: That's all the questions I have.

MR. JONES: Ms. Dragon. Dr. Dragon.

LESLIE DRAGON, having been duly sworn, was called as a witness on behalf of the Defendant, and testified as follows:

DIRECT EXAMINATION
BY MR. JONES:

Q: Good morning. Speak up so the court reporter can hear you. I know I'm bad about mumbling. She always fusses at me. Would you state your name and how you are employed?

A: My name is Leslie Dragon, I'm a house call veterinarian.

Q: And how long have you been a veterinarian?

A: I've been a veterinarian for 19 years.

Q: Are you familiar with the Dogs Deserve Better facility and Ms. Thayne?

A: I am.

Q: How long did you work for them?

A: I started there probably at the beginning of July.

Q: Of this year?

A: Of this year. Yes, of this year.

Q: So did you ever treat the dog Jada for any issues?

A: Not Jada.

Q: Did you see—when you would go to the facility, would you go for just one specific dog, or while you were there would you observe—

A: I would observe all the dogs that are there, but if one needed—more than one needed any kind of treatment, a vaccine or anything, I was there to take care of everything while I was there.

Q: And did you observe anything that caused you any concern for any of the dogs that were there?

A: Absolutely not.

Q: Did you observe anything that you believed to be improper?

A: Absolutely not.

Q: You're not supposed to ask a question that you don't know the answer to, but are you under any type of mandate to report abuse if you see it?

A: Not mandate, but I mean morally I would certainly report abuse.

Q: I don't know how much you could hear sitting there. If a dog is in a fight or scuffle with another animal, when should a veterinarian be consulted for care? What should someone look for?

A: Bleeding. Any obvious wounds. Deep wounds. Bleeding. Pain. Crying. Things like that.

Q: Something where a nip or a bite can be treated with peroxide and antibacterial—

A: Yes, a minor injury, absolutely.

Q: And I'm sorry, when did you say was the last time you

were there?

A: I was just there September 4th. Wasn't it the 4th? I believe it was the 4th.

Q: All right. So after Jada had been removed?

A: Yes, after she had been removed.

Q: But you had been I think you said somewhere in July?

A: Yes. The beginning of July, I believe it was—I think July 11th was the first time I was there.

Q: And then is this the second time you've been there, the September date?

A: The third. The September date. I've been there three times.

Q: All three times everything looked okay?

A: Absolutely great. Clean. Absolutely clean. Dogs looked fabulous. Very healthy, very well fed, very well cared for. Lounging around on beds that she has in the kitchen, all around the place, with blankets and toys. They looked very well cared for to me.

MR. JONES: Thank you, Doctor. Answer any questions Mr. Hefty or the Court may have.

CROSS-EXAMINATION
BY MR. HEFTY:

Q: Dr. Dragon, if a dog were crated for 20 hours a day, do you think that would be cruel treatment?

A: Yes.

Q: And if a dog were maced constantly?

A: Constantly, yes, that would be cruel treatment.

Q: And did you ever actually—were you ever asked to examine Jada?

A: No.

Q: So you never really did?

A: No, not Jada.

MR. HEFTY: That's all the questions I have.

MR. JONES: Nothing further of the doctor.

I believe we'd rest, Judge.

THE COURT: All right.

MR. HEFTY: Your Honor, I'd like to renew my request to have a continuance to next Tuesday to have another witness testify.

MR. JONES: Judge, I have to object to that.

THE COURT: I don't particularly like to overrule it, but I think the statute—I think I would always put in there for good cause shown, but I don't see it. It says "shall" have a hearing. If a statute is going to have any meaning, it's got to have full meaning for everybody. Unfortunately it does put a burden on you, 10 days upon the seizure. And you might say, well, you can wait to seize the dog. Well, that's not a good answer. If the dog is extremely underweight you can't wait to seize the dog, and I fully understand that. So you know—But I think a letter to the General Assembly might help us out on that one. I don't like the idea—I've never been a fan of—I won't say trial by ambush, but I will say of both sides having adequate preparation. But I'm going to have to deny your motion. I think we have to have the hearing on this matter, and I think the hearing is a substantive hearing.

So now, having said that, you have rested, both sides have rested. Let you go first on the argument.

MR. HEFTY: Your Honor, based on Officer Terry's testimony of having observed the dog and the marks on the dog, I think it's evidence of cruel treatment and not being provided adequate care. That's all the evidence we have today.

THE COURT: I understand.

MR. HEFTY: I think it's sufficient.

[Me: Baha. Yeah...not.]

MR. JONES: Judge, the testimony from Officer Terry was on September—I'm sorry, July 20th she observes the dog, and there were no marks. On August 24th there were some marks that were healed. So in the course of a month a mark was put on which healed, which I don't know that—the doctor's indicated that minor wounds don't require veterinarian care. And Ms. Thayne has testified that they give care when it's needed. You can see what the dog looked like in November when they acquired it, and the pictures of the dog the day it was seized, and again I can only let the pictures speak for themselves. But in this particular case I understand there may be something more, and Officer Terry is left with what she can testify to, but in this particular case the evidence before you is that this dog has not been cruelly treated or failed to provide adequate basic care. The doctor says everything was lovely.

THE COURT: Last shot.

MR. HEFTY: Nothing further.

THE COURT: There's an old expression, a picture is a thousand words, and I'm looking at the pictures of November 6, 2011. This dog was in rough shape. I see scars, pretty bad scars all over the forehead, if you will, then those underneath the back—I guess that's left leg.

Bad scar up under the body on the upper part of the leg. You see scars on her rump, or rear end if you will. These are pretty nasty scars. You said she may have been thrown out of a truck. I don't know. But then I'm looking at pictures, I guess that's about 10 or 11 months later, on August 27th, that looks like a very healthy dog to me. I've unfortunately been involved in a lot of dog cases and I've seen a lot of pictures.

Quite frankly you see the picture and that's the end of it. Count the ribs, scars all over, malnutrition. I'm sure you have, too. Yet this dog—and everybody agrees these pictures are accurate. They're presented as evidence. Nobody's disputed them. And all the scars are gone. This dog looks like it's done an amazing job of being healed. I looked at this full frontal face and I can't find any evidence that these scars that were there just 10 months before, if I didn't know that they had been there before I wouldn't see it.

So the veterinarian—and I'm sure she's a sworn professional, sworn in under oath, professional person. I can't—I've had very few vets in my life that didn't love animals, or they never would have been a vet in the first place. It's almost impossible to be a veterinarian without loving animals. That's almost what always draws them. And I feel comfortable that the doctor would have said no, the dog's being treated terribly, and in all my cases before they've always been a witness for the Commonwealth.

In this case I just see pretty strong evidence—or let me

just say this, a very clear lack of evidence—that this dog has been cruelly treated. So I'm going to deny the petition. And of course I think the disposition once I do that is order that the dog be returned to the rightful owner. Obviously if you receive new information, or there is other treatment, you-all can bring another petition at any time. You know, and maybe there's some evidence. And I know you're handicapped a little bit. Maybe there's something the Court doesn't know. The Court has to rule on the petition and the pictures and the evidence and so forth, so I overrule the objection and order that the dog be returned to the owner.

OFFICER TERRY: Can we ask that we have until Friday to return the dog?

[Note: We theorized that Andrea may have taken Jada out of state, which is why she asked for more time. To get her back.]

THE COURT: Is there—why do we need three days?

OFFICER TERRY: I just want to get him vet checked one more time before he leaves so I'm not accused of doing anything to the dog.

[Note: Well, she was a girl, not a boy. And, I believe Tracy Terry was lying there.]

THE COURT: Mr. Jones?

MR. JONES: They want the dog back. They've tried to see the dog. It's not at the pound.

THE COURT: I don't really—I will tell you what I'll give you. This is what, 11:00 on Tuesday? I'll give you until 5:00 tomorrow afternoon.

OFFICER TERRY: Thank you.

THE COURT: The dog should be returned by that time.

[Note: Oh, THANK DOG.
I've never been so grateful in my life.]

Jada takes a doggie bubble bath in Vick's Jacuzzi tub when she comes home.

CHAPTER THIRTY-NINE:

Jada Takes a Bubble Bath, and DDB Gets our First Bequest

I just couldn't believe it! The judge hadn't been in their pocket, and it appeared they were prize-winningly among the worst framers in history. Tracy Terry had shown up at a hearing they attempted to keep from happening with zero witnesses and zero evidence.

Nice.

Of course, she implied that Jada had been attacked sometime between her first visit on July 20th and her next visit on August 23rd. If the dog had injuries that had "miraculously healed" without the intervention of a vet (so that she somehow

199

looked exactly the same both times Terry was there . . . it's a MIRACLE, folks!), then why seize her?

Nothing they did made any real sense.

She also implied that I'd been pepper spraying the dog(s), for fun and kicks I suppose. If that were the case, it couldn't have possibly occurred anytime in the previous ten days, since I was out of the country. Not only that, but if she were charging that I'd forced the employees to pepper spray dogs for my entertainment, why weren't they testifying for the commonwealth instead of me?

There was neither logic NOR a shred of truth behind their arguments. Forget about actual evidence.

I was relieved and ecstatic, but even more angry. How dare they! If it wasn't obvious before, it was blindingly obvious now that it was all just a smear campaign. The fact that they didn't even bother with fabricating evidence was both a huge relief and a puzzle. Why, if they were going to frame me, didn't they do an adequate job of it?

I finally realized evidence didn't matter.

Surry County didn't care if they won the case. The accusation was enough to destroy me, hopefully Dogs Deserve Better too, and force us from the county. The media hopped on the salacious story just as they'd hoped, and I was painted as a villain—now I had to spend time and money in court for even a chance at clearing my name.

Meanwhile, I would be so busy fighting for my own freedom I'd have no time or energy to ensure Deana Whitfield paid for her embezzling.

Win/win for my accusers.

Now I was left to pick up the pieces of my reputation, my organization, and the home for our dogs. The accusation itself was enough to dry up donations, and I didn't blame the donors. Who wants to support an organization that bills itself as fighting for the rights of dogs when the founder is accused of hurting them?

I wouldn't donate either.

For the first time, I had serious doubts as to whether we

would survive this crisis.

Dog caretaker Corrie bakes Jada a doggie cake all her own to celebrate her return.

When officer Tracy Terry brought Jada back from wherever they'd stashed her the next day, our dog looked a little worse for wear. She'd lost a couple pounds, and her fur wasn't as shiny as it'd been the day she was seized. But she was as happy to see us as we were to see her, and we quickly rustled up a little "Welcome Home" party for her.

We made signs, Corrie made a special doggie cake just for her, and—for the ultimate in fun—Jada got her first spa treatment: a bubble bath in Vick's former Jacuzzi tub!*

If you're wondering—like we were—why the commonwealth hadn't brought a vet as a witness to the hearing, we would only find out much later why that was: because the vet's report only showed Jada as having a stomach rash, which she was prone to. We'd treated her for them before.

Their vet had likely refused to state that there was any cruelty involved, so he or she would prove useless to their campaign against me.

---

* Watch the video of her homecoming at https://youtu.be/OXKrhwYd1qY

God forbid they actually drop the charges. I wasn't Michael Vick, after all.

In a stroke of divine intervention, our first bequest arrived in the mail shortly after getting Jada back—to the tune of $151,001.97—when we, along with 24 other animal organizations, were named in the will of a gentleman named Ransom T. McCarty from California.

I sat and cried when the check arrived, I was so grateful to this man I'd never met but who had been so generous to us. With the false charges putting a damper on donations, each month I had the added stress of wondering if we could pay the mortgage and our staff, let alone run our vet care and other activist programs to raise awareness for chained dogs.

But now, because a windfall had come at the exact moment it was most needed, I could breathe a little freer. I knew we could now keep a roof over our rescues' heads for the immediate future, pay the help we so desperately needed, PLUS set up the veterinary care program I'd devised for chained dogs nationwide.

Maybe the world wasn't so horrific after all.

Cute little Scooter in his Christmas outfit. Something tells me he wasn't totally impressed.

CHAPTER FORTY:
Our Second Christmas in the House

*T*hat Christmas we were a small staff of five—employees who'd been through the worst with me, and still believed in our work enough to stand by my side.

Even though Commonwealth Attorney Gerald Poindexter had refused to drop the charges after we got Jada back—which speaks volumes in and of itself—and even though those charges still hung over my head, I was immensely grateful to have help for the organization and the dogs that winter.

I didn't feel so alone.

I hoped that maybe 2013 would be a better year for us, and I wanted to be sure the staff knew I valued them; just before the official holiday I took them out for a Mexican lunch during doggie nap time, and then we celebrated with a small onsite party afterward.

Admittedly, I got a little teary-eyed as I thanked these folks for being there; thanked them on behalf of the organization, me, and the voiceless we served—the dogs who were lucky enough to join us this Christmas, in a warm home and with their own gifts to open on Christmas morning.

I was full of hope. Maybe things were finally looking up?

Nationwide that year we continued our Holiday "Sponsor-A-Formerly-Chained-or-Penned-but-Now-Free-and-Lovin'-Life" Foster program, writing the following Thank You to our supporters:

> Let's face it, our dogs come from nothing. They sleep in the dirt, eat in the dirt, and live in the dirt. When they are lucky enough to be rescued and become part of the DDB Sponsor program, we do our very best to meet their needs—giving them vet care and inside foster homes with love, good food, and plenty of fresh water while they wait for their new homes and families.
>
> Except, there's one thing that we normally don't get to do due to financial constraints: PAMPER THEM!
>
> That's where you come in . . . . Each Christmas our wonderful donors and supporters conspire to make this the first and best holiday of our new rescues lives . . . you all send presents, you sponsor dogs, and then together we spoil them rotten. AND THEY LOVE IT!
>
> For the Fourth Year in a Row, A Very, Very Special Thanks to "Santa Paws," an anonymous donor who matched $5000 of our Holiday Dog donations! We are so grateful to her for her wonderful generosity. As a result, we were able to provide 61 $100 gift cards, one for EVERY dog in the DDB Foster program!
>
> Here's to you "Santa Paws."

Polly and Nala proudly show off their home, spotless and cozy!

CHAPTER FORTY-ONE:
The Case Against Deana

Our embezzling case against Deana had hit a roadblock, in the form of, you guessed it, Gerald Poindexter.

After Sheriff Back from the Surry County Sheriff's office turned the case over to the state police, I was contacted by an officer named Shawna Griffith.

I sat down and met with her, discussing the entire situation and what had happened. Upon looking at the evidence of Deana's paystubs, the officer told me she believed it to be a pretty cut and dried case. She then worked with DDB Treasurer Deb Carr to get the remaining information she needed.

By October, Officer Griffith had finished her case writeup

and submitted it to Poindexter for prosecution.

From: Tamira Thayne
Sent: Tue 10/16/2012 1:20 PM
To: Griffith, Shawna E., SA
Subject: Are Whitfield's charges with Surry County?

> Hello, Ms Griffith,
> Can you tell me if the charges against Deana Whitfield are with Poindexter and Surry County now?
> Thank you.
> Tamira Thayne

From: "Griffith, Shawna E., SA
Subject: RE: Are Whitfield's charges with Surry County?
Date: October 19, 2012 at 10:39:38 AM EDT
To: "Tamira Thayne"

> Ms. Thayne,
> My report has been submitted to Mr. Poindexter.
> SAA Griffith

From: Tamira Thayne
Sent: Fri 10/19/2012 11:09 AM
To: Griffith, Shawna E., SA
Subject: Re: Are Whitfield's charges with Surry County?

> So if he approves charges would he send you out to arrest then?

From: "Griffith, Shawna E., SA"
Subject: RE: Are Whitfield's charges with Surry County?
Date: October 19, 2012 at 2:36:12 PM EDT
To: "Tamira Thayne"

> Once Mr. Poindexter makes a decision on what charges, if any, will be placed, then he will decide if this case goes to a

grand jury or if I obtain warrants. If this case goes to grand jury and if the grand jury returns a true bill, then any law enforcement officer can make the arrest after the indictment is issued. If Mr. Poindexter asks me to obtain warrants and if a magistrate issues warrants, then once the warrants are obtained, any law enforcement officer can make the arrest.

I waited. And yet, as the new year arrived, we'd heard not a word about Deana's case. It had gone "poof", just like the two Vick dogs that ended up in the Surry County shelter.

I shouldn't have been surprised, given the level of corruption coming out of Poindexter's office, but since the embezzling was so obvious, the case against Deana should have been a no-brainer to prosecute.

Deana soon claimed online that she'd been contacted by Poindexter's office and informed there would be no charges against her. Surprise!

It appears the real criminals do indeed stick together.

This precious Valentine needed no words.

CHAPTER FORTY-TWO:
A Little Valentine Love for Chained and Penned Dogs

That February, as we'd been doing since 2005, thousands of Valentines were enroute to their destinations all over the world, and our phone had started ringing off the hook with requests (some not so nice) to remove addresses from our database.

In contrast, we received two phone calls that made the year's campaign worthwhile and provided hope for the future of backyard dogs in America.

A woman from Roanoke called to thank us for the information and said she didn't realize how bad chaining was for her dog. She removed her immediately and took her inside!

A second caller from western Pennsylvania informed us they too had freed their German shepherd from the chain. When we reported these successes on our Facebook page, another supporter wrote: "Keep pushing. It does work. Y'all sent one to a neighbor of mine last year, and the dogs were let out of their pens into the big backyard that same day never to be locked up again. Thank you!"

Break the Chain, Not the Heart God Gave Me. Only a child could at once be so pure and deep.

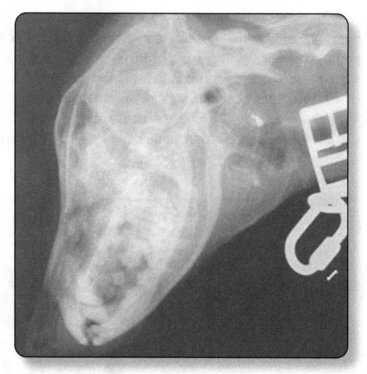

All the white dots are bullet fragments.

CHAPTER FORTY-THREE:

Surry County Dog Shot in the Head
Animal Control Fails to Investigate

*J*ust before we were due back in court on my charges, more evidence of Surry County animal control's mediocracy surfaced: a dog in the county was shot in the head and left for dead.

As luck would have it, the injured dog wandered into the yard of one of our dog caretakers, Jay Gunn, who immediately called me. "Boss, I have a situation here. A dog showed up on my doorstep, and she's hurt pretty bad. She's bleeding from the nose, and I'm not sure what to do."

I was out of town, but gave him the green light to get her whatever care was needed. "Yes, take her to the vet ASAP! Give me a call when you find out more, please."

Jay called me later, reporting, "According to the vet, the bullet fragmented upon entry into her snout, and sprayed all the way through her bones and into her neck. Every spot you'll see on the x-ray shows the path of the bullet into her skull."

The vet initially suggested that euthanasia might be the best option, as there was no way to operate. But the poor girl didn't belong to us, and we didn't feel comfortable making that decision. Not only that, but she was alert enough that she deserved a fighting chance. We went to the media with the story, seeking any information on her, and Laia's guardian stepped forward.

Tracy Terry was interviewed, too, and told the media that "they would investigate to find out IF cruelty was involved." If? A dog took a bullet to the bridge of her nose and she wondered IF—just maybe—there was cruelty involved?

Were we living in the twilight zone in Surry County, where up was down and down was up? I was beginning to think so.

The emergency vet told us if the pellets in Laia's head and neck moved they could kill her, but we felt it was a risk worth taking. Because by some miracle, and thanks to quick action on the part of DDB and Jay in getting her care, Laia was back home with her guardian again in a matter of days; we even built her a fence so she didn't wander off again.

In speaking to Laia's caretaker, the woman told me, "I suspect an old boyfriend did it; but the animal officer only spoke to me once, very briefly, and didn't seem like she cared about getting to the bottom of it. She's never contacted me again."

Tracy Terry never picked up the dog's x-rays from our offices at DDB, either.

Here Surry County seemed to have a cut and dry case of cruelty on their hands, yet they showed no interest in the actual pursuit of justice for the dog and her family.

By mid-2013 we had our very own sign and everything.

CHAPTER FORTY-FOUR:

We're Paid in Full, And Create a $30,000 Vet Care Fund for Chained Dogs

By March of 2013, we'd received our second bequest, this time from the estate of Peggy & Eric Leiber—the creator of "Love Connection", a TV show that ran from 1983-1995. Thanks to their generosity to us and many other nonprofits through their celebration of the arts and animals, we were able to pay off both mortgages for The Good Newz Rehab Center. *We were, not even two years in, debt-free!*

We also purchased the acre next door for a cash deal of

$16,000, upping our holdings to 16 acres and creating an additional buffer zone between us and the neighbor to the right.

The 15 acres and 4600 sq. ft. building had been purchased in May 2011 for the sum of $595,000. We raised approximately $180,000 for the down payment, ending up with two mortgages for the remaining $415,000. **This was all now paid in full.**

I loved the irony that the county tried so hard to get rid of us, and yet the universe provided a free and clear home for our dogs instead.

We also added an additional $10,000 to our Hero Fund, for a total of $30,000 in grant money to provide spay/neuter and other vet services for chained and penned dogs rescued by citizens nationwide.

LISTENING IS JUST THE BEGINNING.™

04/13/2013

DOGS DESERVE BETTER INC
C/O TAMIRA CI THAYNE
1915 MOONLIGHT RD
SMITHFIELD VA 23430

RE:

Dear Valued Customer:

Thank you and Congratulations! Enclosed please find the documents pertaining to your loan, which is now paid-in-full. Thank you for allowing us to service your loan, and we hope you will consider us again for any borrowing needs you may have in the future.

If you have any questions or concerns, please contact your relationship manager or call us as 1-800-FULTON-4. You can also email us via our website at www.fultonbank.com.

As a reminder (and if applicable), please contact your insurance company and have our bank's name removed from your policy, now that your loan is paid-in-full.

Thank you for again for allowing Fulton Bank, N.A. to be your financial service provider.

Sincerely,

Patricia L Lessig
Loan Operations
(610) 332-7373
Fax: 800-755-1664

The organization was now debt-free!

"We don't care about no stupid hearings. Except for what we're hearing down here. Come out!"

CHAPTER FORTY-FIVE:

My Day in Court

"As the dog lay on the ground fighting for air, Quanis Phillips grabbed its front legs and Michael Vick grabbed its hind legs. They swung the dog over their head like a jump rope then slammed it to the ground. The first impact didn't kill it. So Phillips and Vick slammed it again. The two men kept at it, alternating back and forth . . . until at last, the little red dog was dead." —Jim Gorant, "The Lost Dogs: Michael Vick's Dogs and their Tale of Rescue and Redemption"

214

Gerald Poindexter.
Dropped.
ALL.
Cruelty Charges.
Against.
Michael Vick.

*P*oindexter never dropped my case, but it was postponed three times, at least two of those without our knowledge. I'd never received a single document from Surry County in regards to any of the cases against me, had never been advised of court dates, etc., and had to rely on my attorneys to let me know when to be there; one time we only found out it was postponed through the newspaper.

Not only is this illegal—even "criminals" are guaranteed proper notice to appear in court—but it made it next to impossible to coordinate witnesses. I've often wondered if Surry County's court was so dysfunctional that they sent no paperwork to anyone, or if this was a tactic Poindexter was using with me to keep us and the media from showing up at the proper time.

Because although he'd ensured the media was there in full force the day I was arrested, I imagined he'd be much happier if members of the press *didn't* show up for court hearings in which they had no evidence to present.

Finally, eight months later, on March 5, 2013, we would go to court for my hearing on the cruelty charges.

Surry County had never allowed us to see any of their evidence against me. Even though the implied allegations—that I was macing and tazing dogs left and right, and crating them 20 hours a day—had been out there for months, we never saw what they were basing these falsities on, or got a chance to line up rebuttal evidence. We were working blind.

I, once again, felt so incredibly alone.

Even though I had Joe, my kids, my mother, and a handful of

good friends who I believed I could trust (absolute certainty had been stolen from me), no one could solve this problem for me. No one could make the agony of what was happening stop, and no one could make it all just go away.

Usually, even though we as humans try everything we can to avoid painful situations, the only way out is to pick ourselves up by the gonads (er, whatever) and push on through.

I steeled myself to face yet another day of shame, another day where anything could happen.

Another day where I would have to face lies and the possibility of them being spread by the media.

I felt I had no control over my life or destiny.

A dog advocate that I barely knew had turned into a lifesaver during this battle with Surry County; Samantha Laine had actively gotten in the ring with me, pushing me to take the hard and difficult measures I needed to save myself.

Throughout my years fighting for chained dogs, I would discover that I was much better at fighting for the rights of others as opposed to my own. When it came to defending myself, I tended toward avoidance; I'd just walk away. But neither was possible now.

I was deep in the doodoo, and I had to dig my way out.

Samantha was a trainer turned rescuer living in North Carolina, and saw immediately what was happening to me. As a result, she researched attorneys, laws, and animal control experts, even hooking me up with Animal Officer Mark Kumpf, who I'd met at a few animal welfare conferences.

Mark agreed to take a look at my case. He came with some impressive credentials, as past president of the National Animal Control Association and HSUS Virginia Humane Officer of the Year in 2007.

As it turned out, Mark had also been involved in both the Vick and the Benny Butts dogfighting cases in Surry County, Virginia, and had seen the shenanigans firsthand when Poindexter got involved in those cases. He had no problem believing I was the victim of a smear, and he agreed to come visit our facility and go over the evidence from our side with me.

The help I despaired of finding had come to me, once again, in my greatest hour of need.

I often wondered how and why the animal control officer, Tracy Terry, had gotten roped into this obviously false case. It had to have started with Gerald Poindexter, but were there others involved too? Was she told her job depended on it?

What was used to force her cooperation?

It turned out she would not be the first animal officer controlled by Poindexter.

In the Vick case, the book *Badd Newz* goes into detail about then-Surry Animal Control Officer James Smith, who'd requested the help of a nearby jurisdiction with more experience, as he was new and unsure of himself. When Chesapeake officers, led by Kathy Strouse, made the case by giving him a laundry list of evidence items, he worked right alongside them, asking questions and cataloging the pieces.

But not long after, Smith walked into a meeting with Poindexter by his side, and when asked by Poindexter if there was evidence of cruelty, he replied, "Well, I didn't really see nothing wrong out there. A couple of bowls were dirty. And they all had food and water."[7]

Poindexter was apparently no stranger to demanding that animal control officers do his bidding. And they toed the line.

We arrived at the Surry County courthouse with a new attorney, Peter Eliades, along with expert witness Mark Kumpf, veterinarian Leslie Dragon, and volunteers and staff who'd agreed to testify and were present during the time in question.

Poindexter immediately attempted to postpone the case

again, which we vehemently objected to. It had already been postponed multiple times, and we'd flown in our expert witness for the second time. This was unacceptable.

As it turns out, their—apparently one and only—witness, former employee Andrea Wheeler, hadn't shown up, once again. I assume by now she'd realized she was the patsy, the one left holding the bag to do Deana's dirty work. She probably had seen my evidence for Deana's embezzling online, and wanted to steer clear of implicating herself in all that. She'd been lied to by Deana, and now she would have to lie under oath, which most people with a living brain are loathe to do.

She would have had to name the times that I'd been cruel to the dogs, and she would have had to have some kind of direct evidence (like, say, an injured dog, perhaps?) to back her up. The smear had gotten out of hand.

So she fled the state instead, with no plans to return.

The judge heard arguments from both sides with regards to postponing the case, and in the end he sided with us.

The commonwealth would either have to present its case or drop the charges.

The courtroom was packed with media and curious onlookers, and all were pretty disappointed when Poindexter chose to do what is called a "nolle pros." There would be no hearing today.

In layman's terms, "nolle pros" meant that they dropped the charges, but reserved the right to refile them again.

In order to keep the smear alive.

Deana sat in the back of the courtroom, with her popcorn and her girlfriend Katie, just waiting to watch the show she'd created for herself to start.

I had mixed emotions; there were intense feelings of relief, of course, yet I was also being deprived of the chance to beat them, fair and square, in a court of law. It was obvious to me that Andrea Wheeler had no intention of showing up. We'd spanked them in court the first time for Jada—the judge declaring "a very clear lack of evidence of cruelty"—and yet they still wanted me to live in fear, to drag it out and threaten me by holding it over my head.

At that moment, any pondering of my mixed emotions would have to wait. I had a job to do now: put on my own case for the cameras.

We invited the media back to our facility at 1915 Moonlight Road, where they could meet our lovely dogs and listen to statements from myself and my two expert witnesses, something it seemed we would be deprived of in a Surry County courthouse.

I won't bother regaling you with my statement, but Mark Kumpf and Leslie Dragon spent a few minutes in front of the cameras, too, giving their perspectives.

Here's what Dr. Dragon said, in full:

"My name is Leslie Dragon. I'm one of several area veterinarians who have provided care for the animals here at Good Newz Rehab. I can tell you firsthand, from all my visits here, that these dogs are nothing but well-cared for, loved animals that have been taken from horrible, neglectful, abusive situations and then very successfully treated and rehabilitated and placed in new forever homes.

"I find what they do here to be absolutely commendable, and I've found absolutely no evidence whatsoever of abuse of any of the animals here by any of the staff members, employees, anybody.

"I think they do a fabulous job, and I think that the accusations presented against her are completely unwarranted. I hope that people will see that. She does a fabulous job; the accusations are false."

Statement from expert Animal Control witness, Mark Kumpf:

"My name is Mark Kumpf. In my regular job, I'm the director of the Montgomery County Animal Resource Center in Dayton, Ohio. I did travel all the way here from Ohio for this case. This is the second time I've been here as an expert witness for the defense in this case. Which is a little unusual, because in my expertise and coming from law enforcement and animal control, generally I find myself on the side of the prosecution.

"In fact, when Surry County prosecuted a former dogfighter, Mr. Butts, about a decade ago, I was an expert witness in Surry Court with Mr. Poindexter prosecuting that case, sitting at the prosecution table. It's a little different being here today on the other side.

"I was contacted by Dogs Deserve Better and Tami Thayne, who I've known for a number of years as well, and was asked to take a look at this case and review the procedures and the evidence. Based on what I reviewed, I'm here today as an expert witness for the defense, and to give my opinion on how this case was handled.

"Unfortunately, we sometimes find that there are cases where the evidence doesn't support the charge, and without the witness who seems to have been unable to make it here twice now, the commonwealth wasn't able to proceed today. . . .

"The animals that I've seen here—and I've had the opportunity to observe how Dogs Deserve Better does business here at the Good Newz Rehab Center—these animals are well taken care of. The staff and the volunteers here conform, at least in my opinion, to all the requirements of the Virginia state code, providing adequate care, adequate exercise, all those elements which are the responsibility of any owner, not just any animal shelter.

"Beyond that, the allegations that somehow these animals have been cruelly treated and neglected or abused, I can't find any evidence of that. Having reviewed the documents and the information provided to me, should this case come forward again, that's going to be the substance of my testimony in court.

"If you abuse an animal, there's evidence. If an animal is, for example, pepper sprayed continually, and having worked in animal control for going on over two decades, we know what that looks like. . . . Pepper spray, or oleoresin capsicum, is used by police departments all over the country and animal control;

it's a nonlethal, inflammatory agent that's used to dissuade an attack.

"I've been here; again, I've yet to see anything that would even indicate to me that the animals here, that that would be required. I've spent most of the time here playing with them actually."

Tracy Terry told the media she was planning to refile the charges.

Dog caretaker Tim with Bella in the field.

Mark Hyre plays with the dogs in our front dog yard.

CHAPTER FORTY-SIX:

We Hire a Director of Operations, & I Get to Move Out!

Joe and I had bought a home in Culpeper County, Virginia, in January 2013, but I was still living at the center more often than not. Even though DDB now had enough staff to get the job done without me, I still felt it was important that someone oversee the operations as often as possible.

I couldn't afford much more to go wrong, and I didn't trust local authorities any further than I could throw them.

In March 2013, Dogs Deserve Better finally hired our first Director of Operations. For almost 12 years I'd tried to do it all, because budget constraints didn't allow me to hire executives to help run the organization.

Things I didn't know how to do I had to learn to do, and areas where I didn't excel I had to at least do a passable job in order to keep Dogs Deserve Better up and running.

I wondered time and again how anyone else starts a non-profit—because surely it couldn't be this hard for everyone?

I'd spent almost two years here getting the center off the ground, and during that time the activist side of our work hadn't gotten the attention it deserved.

Thanks to the second bequest we'd received, funding was available to put an executive into place who had the skills needed to run the center, the small staff, and daily operations of the organization, while I focused on awareness and activist campaigns.

I couldn't wait!

DDB soon welcomed Mark Hyre, a 50-something fellow Air Force veteran from Florida, as our new Director of Operations. Mark and his girlfriend Laurel moved to Virginia, where they took over the big suite that used to be Vick's—yes, the one with the crooked toilet (I wouldn't miss it).

I used the guest room across the hall when I stayed onsite.

Mark came from a real estate and community management background, but always wanted to make a difference for dogs, so he was delighted to make the switch into the nonprofit world. I was happy to have someone with a knowledge of building and facilities, as I found the whole side of managing the center quite overwhelming.

Mark quickly got the roofs and doors on the sheds fixed from where they'd taken storm damage, removed any remnants of debris from our field, coordinated our new vinyl fencing for the dog yards, and ordered our sign for the front of our property.

I was excited to have him as part of the team.

I spent March and April working with him and getting him trained in how the organization operates, and then I was finally free to go back to where my forte lies, while continuing as CEO of the organization.

Everything seemed to be going smoothly on the surface, but

Mark, like Elaine, was also an alcoholic; he assured me he was and had been on the wagon for a very long while.

Bianca took her freedom very seriously!

Looking back, I can see that I felt a certain uneasiness with him in place after what happened with Elaine, but I told myself not to allow that bad experience to affect my judgment of Mark and his capabilities.

Not everyone fell off the wagon so spectacularly, and surely it wouldn't happen again, right?

Only time would tell.

Cody runs with the dogs in the field.

CHAPTER FORTY-SEVEN:
Speaking with Poindexter . . . About Deana's Case

After I was "free but not free"—with their charges dropped but still hanging over my head—I called Poindexter to discuss Deana's charges. He really should have recused himself from her case, since he was already busy ruining her boss's life. He had no business NOT doing so, but when you're running a smear (and running the show in Surry County), the rules don't apply.

I would send the following email to my lawyer about the conversation:

225

- Poindexter is either really stupid, or really good at playing stupid.
- First he told me that he only prosecutes the charges, that whether to charge her or not has nothing to do with him. He said he's never seen the charges.
- Said why didn't I have the magistrate file them. I told him we gave them to Surry County Deputy Back, who gave them to the state police.
- Then he said they are on his desk, but he's not the one who decides.
- Then I read him what the state police officer, Shawn Griffith, wrote me via e-mail:

> "Once Mr. Poindexter makes a decision on what charges, if any, will be placed, then he will decide if this case goes to a grand jury or if I obtain warrants. If this case goes to grand jury and if the grand jury returns a true bill, then any law enforcement officer can make the arrest after the indictment is issued. If Mr. Poindexter asks me to obtain warrants and if a magistrate issues warrants, then once the warrants are obtained, any law enforcement officer can make the arrest."

He said yeah, that's true, but he hadn't had a chance to look at them yet. I said you've had them since September. He said that's not true.

- He then asked me about our evidence, I told him it was a cut and dry case of her padding her paycheck, an obvious paper trail. He said, "Do you think it was intentional." WTF?
- Then he said he'd look at them, and to give him 30 days. But he may need to have someone else prosecute that case because he's prosecuting me.

I was pretty sure I'd just gotten a taste of an official Gerald Poindexter runaround.

It was heartbreaking seeing Chippy on that chain day after day.

CHAPTER FORTY-EIGHT:

Rescued! A Dog We'd Been Watching on the Chain Since our Arrival

hippy was the one who almost got away for us at the Good Newz Rehab Center, but we were finally able to rescue the old boy—a 12-year-old lab/sharpei mix who lived just two miles from our facility.

In chained dog rescue, there's always that one dog who sticks in your craw . . . for staff at DDB, that dog was Chippy. We'd watched him since moving to Virginia two years earlier, and when we drove past his ring of dirt, he'd either be standing forlornly looking toward the house, or laying in his doghouse with just his nose sticking out.

He was loved from afar.

It was obvious the dog was old, and his caretaker wasn't breaking any laws. He had to be willing to give him up to rescue for Chippy to be free, but the man just wouldn't say yes.

We were worried Chippy would die out there on the end of that chain, having never known true love or what it's like to live inside with a family.

The Surry County SPCA (not affiliated with Surry County Animal Control) had been trying to free him from his chain for years. DDB, working in conjunction with the SPCA, convinced the caretaker to accept a fence for Chippy as well as trips to the center to run in our large fenced area. It was progress.

But then we got a miracle! When Mark and I drove over to bring Chippy to the field to run for the first time, his caretaker changed his mind and allowed us to rescue him instead! Both groups celebrated the fabulous news, and got to work bringing him to health.

Chippy was heartworm positive and blind in one eye, but nothing kept him from enjoying each and every day of his new-found freedom—as every dog deserves.

We took chain, doghouse and all, just in case the owner became tempted to chain another dog. It was a glorious day.

After that, when we drove by and reflexively looked over for Chippy, he wasn't there. **Because he was with US.***

Chippy finally got to lift his head to the breeze and know the feeling of freedom.

---

* **Watch the video of Chippy's rescue at** https://bit.ly/2NHVUvs

An overview of our new vinyl fenced yards. Photo by Rita Thomas.

CHAPTER FORTY-NINE:

The Center Upgrades to Vinyl Fencing

When we moved to the Good News Rehab Center, we couldn't afford the solid vinyl fencing we knew we'd eventually want for more curb appeal while keeping our dogs secure and happy at play in their yards.

But thanks to Central Bark Doggie Daycare Inc., who raised $10,000 toward the panels, we soon revamped our dog yards in a way that was both aesthetically pleasing and safer for our dogs. We raised the remaining $8500 by selling panel sponsorships to our supporters, who in return got their own **special "in memory or in honor of" plaques** which were affixed to the panels.

Despite all efforts to the contrary, DDB had moved forward, and our beautiful new fencing was just one more sign of our progress in bringing our facility to fruition.

Hunger Strike Day 30. Note Poindexter in the background, right.

CHAPTER FIFTY:

I Fight Back, Part 1 . . .
Enter the Hunger Strike

"IF YOU WANT TO GO INTO THE ARENA, YOU HAVE TO BE PREPARED TO TAKE A PUNCH. BUT YOU ALSO HAVE TO BE PREPARED TO THROW A PUNCH."—HOUSE SPEAKER NANCY PELOSI, THE LATE SHOW, OCTOBER 31, 2019

I was sick and tired of the harassment I'd been undergoing in Surry County, and there was no end in sight as their threats to recharge me still hung over my head. By now it had been almost two years of nonstop torment because I was dumb enough to buy Vick's house of horrors. It was time to fight back.

I was a big fan of the courage shown by the suffragists, and my favorite movie about the battle for women's voting rights was "Iron Jawed Angels", a 2004 HBO documentary starring Hilary Swank. Watching that movie never failed to fire me up, and made me yearn for that same level of justice for chained dogs.

But now I needed to put that desire for justice to work for myself, too.

It was obvious that the county had no respect for me as a human being, or Dogs Deserve Better for that matter. We weren't being granted our basic rights to a peaceful existence in the county, rights that should be readily available to all who harm no one.

Dogs Deserve Better was the victim of the crime of embezzling, and I was the victim of collusion on the part of the embezzler and leadership of Surry County. Simple as that.

Yet we were the ones treated as criminals.

I decided to take a page out of the suffragists' playbook.

Women in America fought for the right to vote for 72 years. 72 years! Can you imagine? Finally, in 1920, the Nineteenth Amendment to the U.S. Constitution was ratified, stating:

> "The right of citizens of the United States to vote shall not be denied or abridged by the United States or by any State on account of sex."

The tool the suffragists employed to get across the finish line was picketing as "Silent Sentinels" in front of the White House, in all weather, and every single day.

When they were arrested and sent to a work house, the women initiated a hunger strike, and were force fed by those in power and control.

In the end, these hardcore tactics finally pushed legislators to do the right thing, in a way that no amount of "be a good girl now and wait your turn" had done for the 72 years prior.

Based on their example, I decided to commence a hunger strike and one-woman protest in front of Poindexter's office, outside the circuit courthouse in the small town of Surry, Virginia.

Most folks don't really get the point of the hunger strike, and I didn't initially understand it either. It seemed manipulative to me . . . as in "give me what I want, or I'll starve myself to death."

But in "Iron Jawed Angels", Alice Paul described the hunger strike in a way that I could understand and get behind. It made sense in the case of an abuse of power by those in control, when there seems to be no legal recourse.

What do you do when the corruption goes all the way to the top?

According to Wikipedia, "Hunger strikes have deep roots in Irish society and in the Irish psyche. Fasting in order to bring attention to an injustice which one felt under his lord, and thus shame him, was a common feature of early Irish society. . . . The fast was often carried out on the doorstep of the home of the offender. Scholars speculate this was due to the high importance the culture placed on hospitality. Allowing a person to die at one's doorstep, for a wrong of which one was accused, was considered a great dishonor."

I was taking the fight to Gerald Poindexter.

I began my strike on May 7, 2013. Using a restaurant-style sidewalk chalkboard, I changed the number for each day of the strike, and set it along the road so passersby could easily see how long I'd been out there. I also created other protest signs that I held as I sat or paced the grassy area.

I set up shop across the street from Poindexter's office, on the lawn outside of the circuit courthouse. Sometimes I was joined by others, but more often than not I was alone.

On day 30 of my Hunger Strike for Justice in Surry County, I started to feel really sick—nauseous, lethargic, uneasy. I couldn't sleep the night before. I wanted to crawl out of my skin, and kept feeling like I had to throw up, but didn't want to because I knew it would be acidic. I'd been drinking 1-2 cups of veggie broth five days a week previously, but had cut that out the week before, dropping back to just water. I had also cut out any and all vitamin drinks or vitamins of any sort that same week.

My husband Joe was spending the day with me, as he was becoming worried for my health. The day was sunny and warm, and between feeling ill already and walking in the hot sun, I ending up collapsing around 4:00 p.m.

A couple hours before I crashed, I started choking and threw up what little water I had in my system.

How Surry County treated its crime victims.

The ambulance came, and I was diagnosed with a weak, high heartbeat, very low blood pressure, heat exhaustion, and dehydration. Upon further examination at John Randolph Hospital in Hopewell, Virginia, it was determined that I had metabolic acidosis, which is what had me throwing up and kept me hospitalized while they sought to reestablish my ph levels in the body.

At the urging of my doctors, family, friends, and supporters, I began eating again in order to regain health to my body. Twelve needle jabs, five bruises, two IVs, and a two-day stay in the hospital later found me at home, recuperating in central Virginia with husband Joe, our dog Sloan, and cats Mitsi, Tuna, and foster kitty Princess Vivian.

While I was out there, Poindexter would tell a local newspaper that I'd probably framed Deana for a crime, rather than the reverse.

He stomped across the road to confront me on numerous occasions, yelling, flailing his arms around, and making ridiculous statements. One time he invited me inside his office to look at the case files the state police officer had created to hold the case against Deana Whitfield. It was in a big black binder, and I was impressed with Detective Griffith's thoroughness. She would have never gone to all that trouble if she thought there was no case.

Poindexter even made me a copy of her tallies for the final amount embezzled: $1006.22.

PAYDATE	ACTUAL AMT OF PAYCHECK	HOURS WORKED/ VAC HOURS	HOURLY WAGE	AMT PAYCHECK SHOULD BE	DIFFERENCE
1/26/2012	767.97	70.00	11.98	838.60	-70.63
2/9/2012	767.97	70.00	11.98	838.60	-70.63
2/23/2012	767.97	70.00	11.98	838.60	-70.63
3/8/2012	767.97	70.00	11.98	838.60	-70.63
3/22/2012	1,005.54	70.00	11.98	838.60	166.94
4/5/2012	1,023.08	70.00	11.98	838.60	184.48
4/19/2012	1,023.08	70.00	11.98	838.60	184.48
5/3/2012	1,023.08	70.00	11.98	838.60	184.48
5/17/2012	1,023.08	70.00	11.98	838.60	184.48
5/31/2012	1,023.08	70.00	11.98	838.60	184.48
6/14/2012	655.50	69.00	11.98	826.62	-171.12
6/28/2012	1,281.00	76.00	11.98	910.48	370.52
					1,006.22

Final tally according to state police officer Griffiths.

The DDB treasurer, Deb Carr, and I actually thought it was more than that, but any amount over $250.00 is a felony in Virginia; Deana was four times over the necessary limit for the higher charge.

It would seem that even though Deana had a criminal mindset, she was not so bright. She was salaried part time at around $15,000 per year. She said she couldn't work full time, because she had to get her son from school every day. Looking back on the whole experience, it now seems obvious that she really didn't want to work. Soon she asked if she could work more hours from home, and I reluctantly agreed, because I'm a sucker like that—even though her track record told me she probably wouldn't actually work those hours.

Deana did payroll for the whole staff, so when she added the extra hours into her paycheck, she undercalculated the new amount with the extra hours. This meant she started with a deficit before the first embezzlement occurred in March 2012. Poindexter pointed to the initial "minus 70.63" and said, "See, she was underpaying herself! There's no embezzlement."

I pointed to the final figure, and rebutted, "Until you get to the bottom, where you can clearly see she embezzled over $1000.00, and the amounts changed with each pay. How does that happen when she's salaried? You're looking at a felony right there."

As the pressure ratcheted up, Gerald Poindexter got so worked up he actually told the truth one day. A DDB supporter and animal advocate Miriam Hayes called him on numerous occasions throughout the month, reading him the riot act for his actions. He always raised his voice with her and then hung up, but one day he screamed, **"You give your friend out there a message from me: tell her we don't want her here."**

Even though his statement was cruel, it was actually a relief—because the truth was finally out there. **I wasn't crazy: everything he'd done had been for a reason—to rid himself and Surry County of me and Dogs Deserve Better.**

At times the fear that I would actually die as a result of the fast haunted me. I remember coming home to see Joe one weekend, and as he slept peacefully beside me, I lay wide awake, frozen in terror that I would soon be dead.

Joe had been pretty supportive (after all, what better way to get rid of your annoying wife!) but most of the DDB followers (and my kids) were angry with me for the strike. No one felt that fighting Surry County was worth losing my life over, and they failed to see the underlying purpose of the hunger strike. It was exhausting having to defend myself to those who believed in our mission at a time I was using all my available physical and mental energy to keep going each day.

The ambulance workers were super nice. Except they felt compelled to lecture me too.

Most told me, "He doesn't care if you die, Tami. But we do. The chained dogs need you. Think of them."

I'd reply, "I never said Poindexter cared if I died. I doubt he's even capable of empathy, myself, and I think he'd gladly dance on my grave—if it didn't point some unwanted attention in his direction. If I died out there, would authorities above him actually look into his actions? Would they find evidence of his collusion with Deana Whitfield? Would they find other evidence of wrongdoing on his part, perhaps in the Vick trials?" I believed the answer to all of these questions was a resounding YES. He knew what he was doing was wrong.

And I was drawing unwanted attention to his actions.

In fact, as I sat there day in and day out, folks from the county started coming by to talk to me, trying to figure out what I was up to. I heard horror stories about what the local court was like under Gerald Poindexter, and heard more than my fair share about the local animal control, too. By and large the consensus seemed to be that Tracy Terry did little to nothing to advocate or investigate animal cruelty in the county. In fact, on more than one occasion, I was told that people just shot dogs they didn't want because she never bothered to show up on complaint calls. It still makes me sad today that the animals suffer so much.

These reports seemed to be born out by her actions in regards to Laia, the dog who was shot in the head and still managed to find her way to Jay's house. To my knowledge, Tracy Terry never investigated or charged anyone in that case, even though it made the local news. If she ignored her job when the cruelty was obvious and highlighted, what happened when the stories got no attention?

The day the ambulance came and loaded me up to take me to the hospital was the day that Gerald Poindexter finally decided to take my mission seriously.

County administrator Tyrone Franklin assured our emissary that he would do all in his power to bring about a favorable outcome to this situation, and Poindexter called DDB Director of Operations Mark Hyre about coming to a resolution.

I knew I should have gone back to my post in front of Poindexter's office and started over again as soon as I was out of the hospital. I had him running scared, and maybe he finally would have followed through with doing the right thing, i.e. recusing himself from Whitfield's case, finding another Commonwealth Attorney to take over that case, and dropping all pretense of refiling charges against me.

I should have finished the mission, even if it meant croaking on Poindexter's doorstep.

I felt like a coward.

As an aside to the hunger strike, I was a vegetarian at the time (I lean further vegan these days), and daily had to watch the pig trucks drive by on their way to the Smithfield, Virginia, slaughterhouse. Having lived in the county for two years, I was no stranger to this sad sight, and I'd already seen way too many of these trucks to allow me to easily sleep at night.

The main street of Smithfield was super cutesy, with shops and adorably painted pig statues lining the sidewalks . . . while the smell of death wafted from the plant just a mile up the road. It was disgusting.

Now I had a front row seat to the suffering of these poor creatures multiple times each day, and it was another cruel reminder of the pain that we humans inflict on the animals of this world. I felt ashamed I'd ever been a part of it.

Across the street from where I sat, there was a roadside seafood store, and I was engulfed virtually daily by the scent of fried fish. As my hunger became exacerbated and the days wore on, I began to dream of eating Kentucky Fried Chicken, which I hadn't done in 11 years. Feeling weak but starved, I finally told Joe "I'm going to KFC as soon as this hunger strike's over."

Joe has never been a vegetarian, but he knew I was very committed on behalf of the animals, and he'd laugh and tell me, "No you won't, honey. I know you're starving right now, and the smell of this food is getting to you. But you'll feel bad if you do that. I'll make you some fake fried chicken when you're done, how about that?"

I'd pout and argue some more, because it turns out starving Tami isn't the most pleasant of people. I truly didn't know if I meant it or not. I just knew I was So. Very. Hungry.

But I didn't.

In the end, I didn't stray from my commitment to the animals, and for that I'm grateful. The last thing I needed was to add some well-deserved guilt on top of everything else.

Surry County never did refile the charges. If the hunger strike accomplished anything, it was to convince them that I was just crazy enough to do it all over again.

They'd finally gotten wise enough to back away from me, very slowly.

Worked for me.

Will got a kick out of being an activist.

CHAPTER FIFTY-ONE

The Teen Who Protested by My Side

I wasn't alone in my pain, and one teen even came to protest with me during my hunger strike. When Will first started volunteering at Dogs Deserve Better, he didn't want to talk to staff. "I didn't feel like I could trust anyone again." But the dogs were different; the dogs he could open up to.

When we first met Will, we saw a typical teenager figuring out how to make his way in the world.

But underneath the facade, Will was suffering. Little did we know the depths of the bullying he had experienced in his local school, where he was falsely accused, harassed, and forced out due to the cruelty of others and indifference of school administration. It's a story playing out all too often across America's stage, and Will was another teen victim of an apathetic system.

Will became so depressed he started cutting himself and acting out in other ways to deal with the emotional pain he was experiencing.

Someone suggested he come out and volunteer at our Good Newz Rehab Center for Chained and Penned Dogs in Smithfield, Virginia, and we welcomed him with open arms. We hadn't had many teens spend time with us at the center, but Will was being homeschooled and needed a chance to open up to others, to learn to trust again.

When Will first arrived, he met formerly-chained dog Chippy and saw the sad photo of him prior to rescue; in Chippy, he found a kindred spirit.

"I could relate to Chippy; the abuse and bullying I suffered deteriorated me and destroyed my self-confidence. I understood how Chippy felt on that chain—I wanted to help him feel better," Will tells us in a YouTube interview about his path to recovery.

Will opens up further about the bullying and false rumors and accusations. "I fell into a deep depression. Some people say ah, depression, you get over it easily. But not after what I went through. When the police show up and go through all your things and people don't like you anymore or even talk to you, it's just so hard. I felt like life wasn't worth being a part of. Even though they didn't find anything when they went through my family's home, the damage was already done; what few friends I had made were gone."

Will quickly bonded with the dogs at Dogs Deserve Better, and they with him. He spent a few days a week working with the dogs and helping around the center, until the old Will was peeking through—quick to smile and laugh and with a renewed interest in life.

Will recognized the parallels between the dogs' rehabilitation process and his own. It gave him hope, and inspired him to help the dogs recover. Best of all, it gave him the courage to embrace his own recovery. What Will had gone through was very similar to what I had endured, and because of that we understood one another. *

---

* Watch his video at https://youtu.be/fT9tn-3v8NM

We blessed the gates, the doors, the interiors, the sheds, and of course the dogs!

CHAPTER FIFTY-TWO:

Blessing and Cleansing the Facility

Although we'd had people sage the building and grounds soon after our move, we decided to hold an actual cleansing and blessing ceremony onsite, hoping to remove some of the negative energy. To be honest, we were ready to try anything at that point!

I wanted the service to be interfaith, because folks of all religious backgrounds and spiritual leanings were invited and welcome. Jay Gunn planned it, and Rev. John Ericson joined us as we spoke, prayed, and used water and sage to clear the area in various locations: inside the facility, at the gate, and back by the sheds where the most egregious harm had befallen the dogs.

We were covering all our bases.

And we blessed our rescue dogs, too—because more than anyone else, they deserved it.

Drew in Mississippi was our lucky 100th satisfied grant recipient.

CHAPTER FIFTY-THREE:
Hero Fund Grants Reach 100th Customer

As soon as we received our bequests, I couldn't wait to get started with an initiative I'd dreamed about for awhile: The Hero Fund Grant Program. Dogs Deserve Better established the fund to provide vet care for dogs rescued from the ends of chains or in pens by other individuals or groups.

Chained dogs suffer in myriad ways, both physically and mentally, but it's rare that they have ever been to a vet, ever received preventative shots, a health exam, or a spay/neuter.

Even though DDB ran our own rescue program for chained dogs, due to space limitations we couldn't take in every dog who needed us.

By extending these health care grants to other groups and individuals who rescued dogs from the pain and suffering that is a chained dog's life, we were able to reach more dogs and

provide not only physical help for the dogs but also relieve the stress that rescuers felt over finding money for vet care.

We started the Hero Fund in October 2012 with $20,000, and were able to add another $10,000 to it from a second bequest and donations in early 2013, for a total of $30,000.

As of late October of that year, the Hero Fund Vet Grants had reached our 100th satisfied 4-legged customer!

Drew finally gets in his own home with a family.

I was excited to announce to our supporters:

"Our vet care grants have filled a much-needed gap in funding for rescue dogs. These dogs, who come from nothing, now have citizens nationwide who are fed up with this horrendous treatment for Man's Best Friend and are doing something about it. **This grant knows no color, breed, or size of dog.** Any rescued chained or penned dog is eligible whether cared for by an individual or an organization."

"**Our lucky 100th grant recipient is a brindle pit named Drew from Meridian, Mississippi.** Drew spent his entire life chained to a tree, living in dust, with only a cracked plastic doghouse for companionship. A woman named Dora worked with Furever After Rescue to bring Drew into a loving home environment where he will be housetrained and adopted into a new and better life. Stories like Drew's and so many others warm our hearts; we are grateful to be a financial support to those who step up to rescue those we have no room for."

I was arrested for protesting in violation of a restraining order. While the dogs suffered inside.

CHAPTER FIFTY-FOUR:

Another Activist Arrest

That December 3-15, 2013, I flew to Washington state to advocate for dogs trapped at a nonprofit "sanctuary." We discovered that a dog rescued by one of our reps had ended up there the year before, and after seeing disturbing photos and news stories posted online by Olympic Animal Sanctuary volunteer Pati Winn, we knew it was bad.

Was Sonny even still alive?

We asked for our dog back, but despite repeated and very public attempts to get information on him, we were continually rebuffed.

We needed to go out there and see for ourselves.

At our facility in Virginia, we'd posted open hours of 10 a.m.- 2 p.m. each day, and appointments could be set for other times. The dogs had nap and quiet time from 2 p.m.-4 p.m., but later or evening appointments were often scheduled for those who worked during the daytime. Shelters in Virginia were required by law to post and maintain open hours, and we adhered to our policy stringently.

Unfortunately, the "sanctuary" in Washington state had no such rules, and wasn't allowing anyone inside. Sanctuary is defined as a place of peace and serenity, but the warehouse at 1021 Russell Road in Forks, Washington, was anything but.

I am still haunted by the memory of this sight: hardened urine crusted on top of the crate.

It was a tale of tragedy for the 125 dogs trapped inside that warehouse, as nonprofit founder Steve Markwell refused to return any of the dogs to the groups who sent them there, groups like ours who believed they were going to an actual sanctuary. Markwell refused entry to all who went to help the dogs, and the dilapidated pink building remained sealed off.

Because Markwell wouldn't speak with us or allow us to see inside the warehouse or visit Sonny, we protested the treatment of the dogs outside in the public domain. Soon, both myself and Robin Budin were slapped with restraining orders in an effort to quell our rights to free speech. I protested anyway the next day, and was arrested for standing up for the dogs, getting a three-hour tour of the Forks City Jail.[*]

I'd instructed Robin to leave me in jail for the weekend, and

---

[*] Video of the dogs crying for help and my arrest at https://youtu.be/E3dobZuVeQE

publicize on our Facebook page and other social media that I was there on behalf of the dogs. That information, along with the photos and video of the dogs that were already circulating, would have gone a long way toward forcing local authorities to take action.

Or forcing Markwell to give up the dogs.

But Robin didn't want to be alone, so she came along and bailed me out that very afternoon. To say I was livid would have been putting it mildly. These dogs depended on us to do our very best for them! And because she was lonely, she disregarded my plan and my instructions to her? I was beside myself.

These dogs were living in the very worst conditions imaginable—way worse than chaining, which I deemed to be unforgivable. A chain would have been a vacation for these poor beings.

No, these dogs spent their entire lives—24/7/365—in a crate. Not even a kennel. A CRATE! They were forced to defecate and urinate in these tiny little spaces, and were fed and given water only once or twice a week, according to all reports.

Photo Forks police files.

They could barely stand, barely move, barely turn around. I could still cry today just thinking about that level of cruelty. From a rescue? Insane.

Now that I was onsite, and had witnessed the complete lack of caregiving with my own eyes, I had zero doubts that the dogs inside that warehouse were suffering—possible dying at that very moment.

To be honest, I'd been hesitant at first about getting involved. The last thing I wanted to do was jump onboard with smearing another nonprofit founder, after the pain and harassment I'd endured over the past two years.

But then I saw the photos.

And they were heart-wrenching.

And then I learned one of our volunteers had put a dog there.

And I knew I would have no choice in the matter.

We were joined by other protesters on most days, all horrified by the treatment.

We'd protested for 4.5 hours the day before, and had seen not a single soul enter the building. Markwell drove by numerous times, his supporters taunted us with signs telling us to go home, and I became even more convinced that something had to be done—this was beyond horrific!

We met with the Forks Police Chief, Rick Bart, at 3:00 p.m. that day. He confirmed that Forks police had planned to arrest Steve Markwell on animal cruelty charges, but he lawyered up and they backed down, making a deal with him and his attorney that he would decrease the number of dogs at his facility to 60.

Markwell had not followed through with this promise.

Our facility held only 14 dogs, yet you would see starting at 8:00 a.m. two employees walking every single dog out to the field where they were allowed to run and play. You would also see the same thing at 4:00 p.m. each day. At least one staff member stayed with the dogs until their bedtime at 9:30 each night.

How could you run a facility with 120 dogs and NO ONE IS THERE? I felt panicked. Something was very wrong.

In the end, the pressure from us and many other groups, the media, and individuals nationwide led Steve Markwell to load all the dogs into a semi and drive them from Forks to the deserts of Arizona, where he released them to another nonprofit.[*]

I rented a van and drove to Arizona to pick up Sonny, only to find out that DDB was denied him, ostensibly due to an agreement with Markwell. We instead brokered a deal for him to go to a New York trainer, while we rescued and drove two of the Devore shepherds back with us to the Good Newz Rehab Center.

Sheeby says "Hey, stop poking me in the eye!" She loved other dogs.

Between daily walks and runs in the field and time with staff and other dogs daily, both dogs were soon playing and Waldo would quickly get adopted. Sheba was basically feral, and spent the next two years at our center, where she enjoyed the other dogs, but had a very hard time warming up to humans.

She would eventually go home with one of the former DDB caretakers, where she was understood and allowed to live out her life on her own terms.

---

[*] For the full story on this case, read *I Once Was Lost, But Now I'm Found: Daisy and the Olympic Animal Sanctuary Rescue*, from whochainsyou.com

Staff member Nicki getting wired up for her speaking part.

CHAPTER FIFTY-FIVE:
"The Lucky Ones" Documentary

In late 2013 Dogs Deserve Better and the Good Newz Rehab Center for Chained Dogs proudly presented a 14-minute documentary showcasing our facility and rehabilitation success with rescued chained and penned dogs.

The film profiled the transition from a house of animal horrors to an elegant estate focused on restoring the dignity of mistreated dogs and preparing them for successful adoption into loving families.

The documentary was written, directed, and sponsored by Margery Gallow, chair of the Orpheus Connection, a Boston-based not-for-profit fund. This fund supports and develops programs for charitable organizations addressing the needs of children and animals at risk.

"GOOD NEWZ: The Lucky Ones" was produced by METRO

Productions of Hampton and Richmond, Virginia.*

As a side note, and fair warning in case you watch it: I can't act. I didn't have cue cards, which I desperately needed, and I kept forgetting my lines! How embarrassing.

Now I know at least one of the reasons I'm not a movie star. There may be more . . .

Rita Thomas also donated a photo session during that time, you see her photos throughout.

Rita captured our pups in all their adorableness.

---

* View the short documentary at https://youtu.be/vq-1KhaLu6E

Hoarding cases are just heartbreaking. Often others interfere before you can free the dogs.

CHAPTER FIFTY-SIX:

One More Hoarding Case

Hoarding of animals has become more prevalent in America in the past two decades, and is indicative of serious mental illness on the part of the hoarder. To complicate matters, the community often protects the individual, and local citizens insist on "helping" repeatedly, even though requested change for the dogs rarely if ever sticks. In the end, these well-meaning efforts only serve to enable the hoarders and exacerbate the suffering of the dogs and other animals who depend on daily care from humans.

Dogs Deserve Better had gotten more involved in dog hoarding cases because these dogs are nearly always confined in ways that are unthinkable to those of us who love animals.

In February 2014, Dogs Deserve Better took on a Virginia hoarding case of 11 dogs trapped in a makeshift dungeon.

After local authorities denied that the dogs were still there, I drove to the location, spoke with the dog caretaker—a squatter on the property where there was no running water or sewage— and obtained video of the dogs, who had spent their entire lives in darkness inside a big box. It took the owner five minutes at three different locations pulling free tarps and boards in order to show them to me.

These poor dogs were desperate to get out.

DDB spent a week in Wythe County protesting local authorities failure of the dogs; however, in the end another group stepped in and spent $7,000 for kennels and a small fence leaving the dogs in better—but still unacceptable—conditions.*

It is, and will always remain, my position that dogs want and need a home and family; building them kennels on the same property, where the neglect can easily continue, just enables the behavior and doesn't give the dogs the happy ending that "Man's Best Friend" deserves.

---

* View the video at https://youtu.be/n3LnyGG9FCl

Sampson looked a little scary, but he was a big mush. I adored him!

CHAPTER FIFTY-SEVEN:

Two West Virginia Pups

A teenager named Leigh Ann in West Virginia was overwhelmed by all the animals in need of help near her. I spoke with her on the phone numerous times, and finally promised I'd do my best to bring her some relief. She loved animals so much, but she had no resources to vet them and no place to put those she rescued.

We pulled quite a few dogs from her area over a two-year period, with two rescues that I became especially fond of.

The first was a huge, gangly black dog named Sampson, who lived chained to an old wooden doghouse like far too many do. Even though it was April, the day was frigid, and snowflakes drifted to the ground as we arrived at the property where he was chained.

He shivered in the cold, his short fur doing little to protect him from the wintry temperatures.

I hadn't gotten to unchain a dog in quite awhile, and I basked in the glorious feeling—it's truly one of the most-powerful highs one can imagine, giving freedom to a dog who has no idea yet what joys await him or her.

Unchaining Sampson was like a "fix" I'd forgotten I needed.

I'd rented a vehicle, and so my plan was to keep it hair-free. I had the back all set up, blankets and netting in place, and THOUGHT Sampson was adequately confined for the trip home.

Wrong.

I'm not sure where the plan went awry, but before I knew it the big lug was sitting in my lap, all 100 pounds of him, and I was struggling not to veer off the road as I cackled.

I was just hoping he wasn't aggressive and he didn't wreck us, a serious concern since he was so large and obstructing my vision. And the roads were slippery.

Sampson in his home, bigger than "his little boy!" So cute.

But he would turn out to be a big love bug. He looked a little scary if you didn't know him, but inside he was all squishiness. He ended up getting a fabulous home where he was the heart and soul for two little boys and their family.*

Poor Maxine was injured and in a pen, but first she was dumped outside a West Virginia coal mine and then attacked by a bear, according to miners who witnessed the event. She was lucky to escape with her life.

---

* Watch Sampson's video at https://youtu.be/TTS1sdQx-Bk

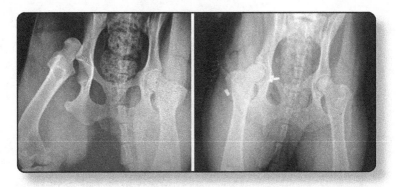

Leigh Ann asked Dogs Deserve Better if we would step for-ward to help her. As soon as we saw the video of her outside the coal mine and knew she was in trouble, we said an immediate YES, meeting Leigh Ann and Maxine at a West Virginia vet where we got the bad news.

Maxine's hip bone was completely out of socket and sitting on top of the bone above. That didn't look good, even to a lay-person. The injury caused her a lot of pain, and she'd scream out whenever she tried to lay down or even go to the bathroom.

On top of that, because she'd been outside in a pen for four days since her attack, it was too late to simply pop it back into place; two vets confirmed it would require surgery.

Maxine was whisked into surgery the day after we got her back to Virginia, and recuperated beautifully, showing no signs of her past injury. The dog was gorgeous, sweet, and quickly found her forever home with a dentist and his family.

Mark petting Sampson in the field, the first day of his arrival.

CHAPTER FIFTY-EIGHT:
Mark Takes a Fall

Unbeknownst to me, Director of Operations Mark Hyre was drinking again. At first he'd been able to hide it, but the problem, as these things do, snowballed over time. Eventually his girlfriend Laurel caught on, and because she was in recovery too and had to protect her own sobriety, she picked up and left.

Mark didn't take the breakup well, and any semblance of sanity quickly left the situation. Most of the staff knew what was going on, but they were afraid to tell me about it, hoping it was a temporary situation and he'd pull himself back together.

When I would spend time at the center, Mark had advance notice that I was coming, and he'd hold it together long enough to get away with it.

Until the day he didn't.

Joe and I had driven to Pennsylvania to pick up a load of dog food from our contact and friend Gordon Bakalar, who volunteered at a mission warehouse and helped us out when he could. We overnighted the food at our home in Northern Virginia, and then the next day, a Sunday, we drove it down to the center.

I texted Mark with our ETA, and let him know to be ready to help us unload. We had to be very careful with our food supply so it didn't attract the field mice into the garage; we were always "all hands on deck" when we picked up a large batch so we could immediately get it stored in rodent proof containers and out of temptation's way.

But when we arrived onsite, dog caretaker Tim L. greeted us instead. He told us that Mark wasn't feeling well and was up in his room. He wouldn't be down. I didn't think much of it at first, so the three of us got the food stocked and all ready to go for the next week. Joe and I decided to walk the property, to ensure everything looked ok and there were no situations that needed to be dealt with.

For some reason, I climbed the ladder to the fighting arena in the top of the largest shed, using the very same ladder terrified dogs were once shoved up, the smell of blood and fear fanning their nostrils. I would go into that space on occasion to remind myself why we were there, what I'd fought for, what I'd been nearly destroyed for.

It was sobering, a memorial to what we were protecting, and what man was capable of doing to the animals—and each other—when left unchecked by the kinder human emotions of empathy and compassion.

Rectangular spaces had been removed from the floor boards to test for blood during the investigation of Vick, and these cutouts dotted the floor in 2-3 places. As I walked the room, I spotted a six pack of beer sitting down in one of the cutout areas, like it was being used as a refrigerator, a hiding place.

My face flamed, and my heart beat faster.

Why? Who?

All too soon the answer would become clear.

I confronted Tim about it, and he denied knowing there was any beer out there. My first thought was that a dog caretaker was drinking on the job, and sneaking out to the shed throughout the day to grab a cold one.

I was worried it was Tim.

I took the beer, and Joe and I packed up and left, discussing the situation on the way out. "It doesn't make sense that it would be Tim," he argued. "He doesn't live there, he can go home and drink whenever he wants. I think it's Mark. Mark has reason to hide his drinking, whereas Tim can drink openly if he likes."

I pushed back against that idea, because I didn't want to face what it meant if it were true. "No, it's not Mark. He's sober, he's told me so many times."

Then the phone rang. It was Tim, and he fessed up to it all. He was afraid he was going to be blamed for it, and that fear was enough to push him to stop covering for Mark. "Tami, I'm sorry to tell you this, but the beer in the shed? It's Mark's beer. He's been drinking for awhile, and that's a big part of why Laurel left.

"He wasn't feeling bad today. He was drunk up in his room."

I was stunned, sickened, and so, so sad.

I cared about Mark. He'd done a lot for the organization, most recently working with an architect to put together the layout for our building extension, Phase Two of our development as the Good Newz Rehab Center.

Plus he handled the staff, the dogs, everything.

Tim went into more details. "He's been asking me to pick him up alcohol when I go out. I think he even used the DDB card to buy beer before, so that Laurel wouldn't see it. He told me he donated the money back to DDB, but still. He shouldn't have done that."

Ugh! What was I going to do?

Selfishly, I was pitying myself, too. I was just starting to come back to life after moving out, and now, without a leader onsite, I would either have to move back or quickly hire someone else.

Joe and I were dumbfounded, emotionally distraught, and stopped at a Taco Bell on our way home to eat our sorrows away. We're emotional eaters, and it occurred to me that whereas Mark used alcohol, Joe and I were more inclined to use food.

One way made you tubby, the other lost you careers you loved.

After doing a little more research to find out the extent of what had been happening with Mark, I knew I had no choice but to let him go. I drove to the center the next week and fired him.

At first he denied it, and I tried very hard to be firm but kind. I felt we were friends, but I knew the organization couldn't handle an executive who was putting his drinking first. We had way too few staff members, and only two leaders. We both had to be on top of our game, and he had lost his way.

Staff was sad, too, and everyone pitched in to help Mark move out and into a temporary situation while he figured out where to go from there.

Once he realized that he wasn't working his way back into his job—that trust would never be regained—the hateful messages from him started. Our friendship was soon gone, too; there were threats to tell Poindexter "something" (would that abuse never end? Would he accuse me of animal cruelty when I was rarely at the center, and he was the one in charge? I was triggered, devastated), and comparisons to Hitler and Mussolini (I can't remember whether I was Hitler or Mussolini, although Hitler sounds more likely).

For the second time, I'd lost a valuable employee to alcohol, and someone I'd considered a friend, too.

I had to pick up the pieces and move on, because the dogs depended on me, and so did the organization.

The cutout where the feds tested for blood in the fight arena. Mark found another use.

CHAPTER FIFTY-NINE:

The One Thing Vick Got Blamed For That He Didn't Do

J shouldn't laugh. I really shouldn't. Except it's hard not to. Within a week after I'd let Mark go, a TV station aired a story about the Vick dogs, seven years later. Their reporter and camera crew had come to the center to interview Mark, and he gave them a tour of the fighting sheds for the piece.

As I watched the story play out, lo and behold—there on the screen in front of me—was that damn beer, sitting in the cutout of the floor, just as it was the day I found it! The camera zoomed in on the blue and silver six pack, and I could hear the reporter asking Mark about it.

"Oh, that beer's been here since Vick had the place," Mark coolly whipped out. "That's Vick's beer."

I was mortified, and again the shame reddened my face. Mark had lied, on camera, and blamed his alcohol problem on Vick!

Then I started laughing, and couldn't stop. I dragged Joe over to watch it, emailed it to the treasurer. "Well," I said, "Now there's finally one thing Vick got blamed for that he didn't do."

Admittedly, it still strikes me funny to this day.

In the years since, I've sought out the interview to watch again online, but have never found it. Maybe Vick's people protested, or maybe it just gradually slipped away into the ether to be replaced by the next story, as these things tend to do.

The "born on" date on the beer was January 2014, almost seven years after Vick had stepped foot on the property.

One of my favorite center photos. Every dog has their own agenda, but they were all together.

The boy scouts completely repainted the sheds and built some fencing too.

CHAPTER SIXTY:

Boy Scout Eagle Project

oy scout Tyler Ducar's family adopted Murray from the Good Newz Rehab Center, and Tyler became interested in helping out our rescue dogs as a result.

Eagle Scout projects are a big deal, and we were honored when Tyler chose Dogs Deserve Better as his project recipient. He brought his troop, the scout leaders, and some friends to build additional fencing for our rescued dogs. They also painted and fixed the fighting sheds as step one in our memorial for those who lost their lives from the abuses of dog fighting, both here and around the world.

There were so many hard days at the center, but seeing these kids all working for the good of the organization and the dogs was a memory I'll always treasure.

Tyler discussing the sheds with his helpers.

Tyler's learning the fine art of fence installation.

Glory in the field with dog caretaker Sherri. Her scarring is very visible.

CHAPTER SIXTY-ONE:

Back to Her Full Glory

*T*he bait dog stood in the middle of the road, refusing to move and seemingly without hope or the will to take even one step more.

It was a cry for help. Will somebody see me?

She was scarred from head to toe, 20 pounds underweight, her fur scarce and dull.

DDB's Amy Hines stopped while everyone else simply drove around her. She gently scooped her up, put her in her vehicle, and drove her right to us at the Good Newz Rehab Center.

The vet determined the pit bull had heartworm and a heart murmur in addition to all her visible maladies.

But she was sweet and gentle, and staff devoted a lot of

time to loving her, bathing her, and caring for her. They named her Glory, because they could see she had once been a beautiful dog, and they knew she could be—would be—again.

Facility manager Julie Sayre reported, "Within only three weeks, Glory has come back to life. Her scars are now almost unnoticeable, and she seems to have no memory of her horrible past or hold a grudge for what was done to her.

Glory and her best friend Dexter take a nap together.

"She even has a best friend now, a little chiweenie named Dexter. He falls asleep on her back like a puppy, but only after they play for hours!"

Glory was our sixth heartworm positive dog in just a month, and that creates a financial struggle for any organization. Very few groups will take in heartworm positive dogs, because the cost to treat them is so outrageous.

Pretty sure our entire staff felt the kind black dog was well worth it.

The "Piano Man" stops by the center and treats us to his mobile music show.

CHAPTER SIXTY-TWO:
I Finally Break Down

By the end of 2014, we were getting the organization back on solid ground after Mark's departure. I finally had a facility manager in place that I was thrilled with, Julie Sayre proving her worth on a daily basis. She'd been hired as office manager months before Mark left, and I was impressed by her steady demeanor throughout the ordeal that soon followed. Julie would eventually move into the upstairs office, and hire a new office manager to take over her former position.

Julie was dedicated, level-headed, and worked extra hours when she needed to, but also made time for herself and her family.

She listened to the staff, but put her foot down when necessary.

She was intelligent, caring, and loved the dogs, the job, and the organization.

My relief was palpable.

At that point, the board of directors voted to allow one of our few remaining area reps, Melody Whitworth, to start an official branch of the organization in Columbus, Missouri. Melody had been with the organization since 2007, and there was no one more dedicated to the cause, or more willing to go the extra mile for the dogs in her local area than she was. She would do the organization proud as leader of a second, satellite facility.

It was only then, after getting two very dedicated women into positions of management, that I officially and finally broke.

I'm not sure why it happened exactly when it did, but I remember the moment clearly. Joe and I had gone to watch a movie at a cinema in Charlottesville, and when we walked out of the theatre, I burst into tears. I was doing those big, ugly hiccupping sobs, the kind you need to do alone in your bedroom and not out in public at the movie theatre.

The movie was about a slacker, and granted, I probably had slacker-envy, but it was so much more than that.

"I just can't do it anymore," I told him.

He was confused, worried I was talking about our marriage.

"What do you mean," he replied, eyes wide.

"I have to leave DDB. I have nothing left to give. It's all gone. I'm 100% depleted, and I'm afraid if I don't get out, there will be nothing left of me to save."

He held me and soothed me, telling me maybe it was time, maybe it was ok for me to go.

My all-time favorite center pic. Heather with one of our puppies still makes me smile today.

Looking back, I can see now that I'd reached the end of my ability to deal with the PTSD I was suffering without help. Every time I would drive to the center, my stomach clenched into knots for the whole 3-hour trip.

It wasn't because of the dogs, and not because of the (current) staff, but because of the place.

And not because of the place, as in our facility itself, which I loved and was very proud of, or even the site where Vick and his buddies killed dogs, which I felt protective of; but the place, as in the county that had done their very best to destroy me.

For no other reason than that I'd dared to buy Vick's property? How cruel.

As I traveled Rt. 10 from Hopewell and into the area, the sign marking "Surry County" never failed to make me physically ill. I would shake the rest of the way to our center.

To this day, I remain sad that I fell apart when I'd finally gotten dedicated staff in place; unfortunately, I believe my body and mind waited for that moment. When there was no one else to shoulder the load, I shouldered it all. When I finally had help to carry it, then and only then did something inside of me feel it was safe to break.

Gideon was one of the worst cruelty cases I'd ever seen.

CHAPTER SIXTY-THREE:

What a Real Cruelty Case Looks Like

*G*ideon came to us from a cruelty case in Ohio, and it's obvious why his owner was charged and ultimately convicted. The rope tied around his neck had embedded, creating a dire medical emergency that nearly cost him his life. The poor dog was skeletal, and as a result of all he'd been through, he was distrustful of new people and reactive to both people and other animals.

The folks at the shelter were worried that he'd be put down because he needed help beyond what they could offer. Two of their staff members drove Gideon and another dog all the way to us at the Good News Rehab Center. We worked with him for quite awhile, and then eventually sent him for advanced training to Mutt Runners in Hampton, Virginia, where he progressed even further.

Gideon and Kit as they bonded and learned to trust one another.

He was eventually adopted by Kit Wilgus, one of the Mutt Runners trainers. Kit reports, "Gideon is now my best dog, hands down. I use his story and background for all my educational work with shelters and in the advocacy world. He is definitely role model material for behavior modification and socialization programs. He will be turning seven years old soon!"

One of Vick's footballs, abandoned in the weeds.

CHAPTER SIXTY-FOUR:

Suing Surry County and How the Three Factions Conspired aka I Fight Back, Part 2

I wasn't leaving, though, before we sued Surry County Animal Control on behalf of myself and the organization. We'd still never seen a shred of their supposed evidence, two years later. After we sued, they stonewalled as long as they could, but were finally forced to hand it over.

I was absolutely stunned and sickened when I saw the lies, the conspiracy, the flagrant abuse of power. Much of the so-called "evidence" came from, surprise surprise, Deana and one of Fiala's sycophants, Carrie Martin, who lived in Indiana and had never been to our facility.

Deana had stopped at nothing to have me destroyed.

Some of the things in the evidence were striking:

On Jul 20, 2012, at 5:37 PM, Tracy Terry <tterry@surrycountyva.gov> wrote

Yes she was careful of what she said in front of the other lady however o did get her to the side and gave her my number and age did call. Everything of course appeared to look fine but I did voice concerns with the office ma..ager as she was the one who kept i, .aking out and lieing to me. The dog with the ear infection has received vet car and anoth dog you mentioned has been adopted. I am going to look into her finacials as to how much vet care has been received this year so far.

Tracy Terry conspiring with Fiala's sycophant, Carrie Martin. Note she says "Everything was fine."

1. Tracy Terry talks about our dog yards and our crates as being inadequate confinement . . . even though our dogs walked twice a day and spent plenty of time out of the crate and in the air conditioned and heated INSIDE of the house. They rotated from dog yard to inside to crate, depending on how well they got along with other dogs. There were doggie doors so they could decide where they wanted to be most of the time. They lived like our own dogs do in our own homes.

2. Right next door to our facility, at the home of Richard Clark, there were 12-15 beagles living in kennels at that very moment. These dogs were sleeping and wading in their own feces, in tiny little pens, yet she had not a word to say about that. How many folks in the county had setups just like the beagles next door? How many dogs in the county never stepped foot inside a home?

3. When Tracy Terry first got the complaints, and not know-ing they were illegitimate, she had a right to come talk to us, even ask to see the dogs. I wouldn't begrudge her that, because I had nothing to hide. BUT, when she clearly tells Carrie Martin in an e-mail dated June 20, 2012 that "of course everything looks fine", that's the end of the ballgame right there. After that point, she no longer had legal justification to darken our doorstep, at least not without a lot more than Deana or Carrie

Martin's word for it.

4. Terry talks repeatedly about KNOWING that Jada was being maced regularly. For one thing, it was Halt! Dog Pepper Spray, (I mixed that up until I learned the difference—AFTER I was arrested.) But an animal control officer should be trained to know that they are two different substances, and shouldn't be continuously using the word mace when it was a pepper spray made exclusively for use as a last resort against dog attacks. More importantly, that allegation was categorically untrue; she did not KNOW anything, except what she was told by Deana. Who was embezzling our money. And who, coincidentally, asked me to buy the pepper spray.

5. Poindexter doesn't show up anywhere in the evidence, at least not what was passed along to us. Except no cases in the county went forward without his approval—see the Vick case or Deana's embezzling case as examples. Like Deana, Poindexter worked from the shadows, pulling the strings of his puppet, Tracy Terry. As Carrie Martin did Fiala's dirty work, so did Tracy Terry do Poindexter's dirty work. And Deana conspired with them all.

From: "Carrie Martin"
To: "Tracy Terry" <tterry@surrycountyva.gov>
Sent: Friday, July 13, 2012 8:19:43 AM
Subject: Re: DDB?

Tracy -

I just found out that the former office manager, Deana Whitfield has been trying to get ahold of you. Can you call her today? 909-

Deana resigned due to issues over the dogs and basic differences with the founder of DDB.

Deana lied about why she left the org—because she was missing too much work—and lied about when she first spoke to the animal control officer. This was right around the time we discovered she was embezzling. Really, what DIDN'T Deana lie about.

In the end, after months of stalling and posturing, we settled out of court for an "undisclosed" amount. I can tell you that it wasn't nearly what we deserved, but it was at least a bare nod toward justice.

What did I do with my share of the money? The first thing I bought was a four-month supply of toilet paper, so I would think of them every time I did my business. Then we took a couple of family trips to the beach, and my kids, Joe, and I each got a little "mad money."

Attorneys Adam Karp and Heidi Meinzer did a fabulous job working the case, but in the end, as far as I'm concerned, the settlement was way too little, way too late.

I was just happy it was over.

If you don't laugh, you'll cry! So I bought some toilet paper in their honor.

There were two fun pieces of evidence in what they passed along, and they give me immense satisfaction, so I'll leave them here with you.

These were letters sent to the Surry County Animal Control after my arrest, letters I would not see for almost two years. Not everyone had the wool pulled over their eyes.

Dear Ms. Terry,

I am writing about the recent allegation against the Smith-field-based rescue group, Dogs Deserve Better, and Ms. Tamira Thayne, the owner. I am a recently retired (June 2012) Navy

Commander and current school teacher who has fostered two dogs for DDB and knows the organization and its people pretty well. Most importantly, I was at the facility on Thursday, Aug. 23, with my 9 year old daughter when your Animal Control officers arrived. I just read in the Virginian Pilot that what your officers "saw" on that same day led to the charges being filed.

What exactly did your officers see that I did not? The public certainly has a right to know.

I speak from first-hand knowledge and will testify to the same if needed. I have known Tami and her organization members to be ONLY loving, kind, and caring to the animals under their care. We were picking up a beautiful shepherd dog, Bandit, for foster that day and saw only all animals in good health, with plenty of water and room for exercise and obviously in good hands. What are the "animal abuse" charges? What is your evidence? And most importantly why did you take Jada? The dog is in great health and has no issues or "danger" concerns. . . . Provide answers asap.

Meanwhile, I am also advising the sheriff, Governor's office and Virginia Police of what I saw and know on this very important situation. This Virginia taxpayer and many others demand a clear explanation of why you acted the way you did, and what basis for your charges of "animal cruelty." It is unreal that such charges could be filed without divulging why and/or on what merit. What country is this?! I look forward to a prompt response to inform all the supporters who are watching this very closely.

Sincerely,
Caroline T.

Although I knew Caroline and she told me she was there that day and willing to witness for me, I hadn't known that she'd written to Tracy Terry. I was touched.

I don't know the author of this second letter, and—full disclosure—his/her letter would most likely be deemed politically incorrect. But for the falsely accused, it remains a delight.

Dear Ms. Terry:

I was dumbfounded what I read about the action you and your group are undertaking against Tamira Thayne. I probably should not have been surprised that a group of under-educated rednecks would try to instigate something so ridiculous after ignoring years of animal abuse and torture that went on at the same site. It is patently clear that abuse was ignored by your offices and the local Barney Fifes, abuse they would have been well aware of given the nature of communication in that part of the country.

But somehow you goosestep against someone who's running what is clearly—clearly—a well-meaning and well-run shelter? How stupid are you people? Do you not recognize that people will recognize this charade for what it is? Unbelievable. And it's unfathomable your offices were not aware of a dog-fighting operation going on there and equally unreasonable to think you are not aware of other such operations in your jurisdiction. We all know there are plenty of other dog-fighting inbred locals you apparently take no ongoing action against.

You might think about doing your job, such as it is, more professionally, if not barely adequately, instead of trumping up charges that are clearly without merit. And don't for a second think that people with a working brain stem don't recognize you doing this when Ms. Thayne was away and couldn't stand up directly to your ridiculously disingenuous tactics. You should be ashamed of yourself, if you have non-fetal-alcohol affected brain cells that allow you to understand common sense. No wonder you're "not talking." Though I'm not sure talking would make you look any more ignorant and slimey than your actions have already painted you.

I'm eagerly awaiting the legal process and the public opinion and press shitstorm that will be coming your way, deservedly so. You are a joke.

Regards,
E. J. F.

Poor Butch was an absolute mess on the chain.

CHAPTER SIXTY-FIVE:
The Last Two Rescues Under My Leadership

"I LOVED VISITING THE GOOD NEWZ REHAB CENTER, THERE WERE SO MANY DOGS TO MEET AND BOND WITH. I REMEMBER WHEN JULIE AND THE OTHER STAFF MEMBERS STAYED WITH ONE OF THE DOGS AS HE LEFT THIS LIFE FOR THE NEXT; THE COMPASSION FOR THEIR CHARGES WAS OBVIOUS IN ALL THEY DID. JULIE EVEN GOT THE TATTOO OF THE ANGEL AND THE DOG. TO THESE DOGS THE STAFF AT DDB WERE RESCUE ANGELS!"—NANCY ROBINSON SELL

*B*utch the chow chow spent ten years on a chain in South Carolina—his long hair matted, his bowls empty, and his life sad and lonely.

That was before rescuers started working with his caretaker, who agreed to release him, but only after asking "Why do you want that old one? Are you going to put him down or something?" **She didn't think he was worthy of a good life or that anyone would want him.**

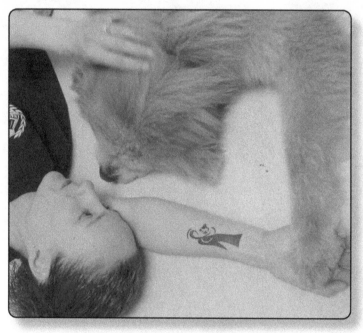

Julie stays with Butch as he comes to his end.

But Dogs Deserve Better felt differently. Every dog deserves some time to feel loved and wanted before the end of his or her life. We wanted Butch to know the life of a "real" dog—just like all the other dogs we'd rescue from chains. So we stepped up to care for him and brought him to the DDB Good Newz Rehab Center until his passing.

Butch was not the only one who got to experience his first taste of freedom that weekend. Misty joined him after her release from her thick logging chain, and brought a tear to staff's eyes as she raced through our fenced field at the Good Newz Rehab Center, experiencing the joy of running free for the first time ever.

Misty's before photo. A despicably heavy chain for a little girl.

CHAPTER SIXTY-SIX:

I Announce that I'm Leaving

*B*elow is the official announcement of me stepping down from Dogs Deserve Better:

Today I announce that it's time for me to pass the baton of leadership of Dogs Deserve Better on to a new director. I founded Dogs Deserve Better in 2002 in Tipton, Pennsylvania, from my home, and together we put the issue of dog chaining on the map.

At that time, no one was taking on chaining as an issue, and I was searching for a way to make a difference in the world. I lived about a quarter mile from a chained black lab named **Worthless, and my suffering over watching his suffering led** me to take a stand against keeping a dog in such a cruel and inhumane fashion in America.

After leading the organization for 12.5 years, and growing it from nothing to a thriving but small facility on the site of Michael Vick's former dogfighting compound in Smithfield, Virginia, I now know that it's time to hand the reins of leadership of Dogs Deserve Better over to a fresh and innovative leader.

A few years ago I was at a conference and a speaker posited that no organization would thrive if the founder stayed involved past the initial phases of growth. At the time I wasn't interested in hearing that, however, I've come to believe that that is true.

I believe it takes an activist to form an organization like Dogs Deserve Better. Someone who is willing to stand up to the abusers and someone who is willing to put him or herself in harm's way to fight for the rights of the downtrodden.

However, I also believe there comes a time in the growth of an organization where a more team-oriented leadership is required.

I want the best for Dogs Deserve Better. I love this organization with my whole heart, and I gave it my all. The organization is like my child—but like any child, there comes a time when a parent needs to let go and allow the child to stand on his/her own two feet.

I am excited about the future of Dogs Deserve Better. **We have built a stronger board in order to provide support for the new director, and between the new director and the board I know we will get our addition built so we can double the number of dogs we serve in the very near future.**

I hope and pray my vision for a state-of-the-art facility on the property will also come to pass in the next few years, where we will house, rehabilitate, and train as many as 50 formerly chained dogs at any given time and ready them for new, inside, and loving families.

I want to thank every single donor and every single employee and volunteer who helped build Dogs Deserve Better from nothing to the wonderful organization it is today.

I send a very special thank you out to a special person, **Deb Carr,** who has truly been the wind beneath my wings for all these years. She has been a sane sounding board too many times to mention in my hours of need, and **she will remain on the board of directors for the immediate future to ensure continuity as we move to an exciting new time for the organization.**

I also send a big THANK YOU out to **Julie Sayre, our facility manager at the Good Newz Rehab Center for Chained and Penned Dogs in Smithfield, Virginia, who I trust to continue to care for our dogs in the way that they deserve.** I thank all the staff and current volunteers, and especially our donors who make our day to day care for abused dogs possible.

For those who have loved and supported me through this journey, I give you my heartfelt thank you. **It has been much harder than I could have ever known, but also more rewarding than I will ever realize.**

And lastly, to the dogs who are still living chained and alone, I'm sorry I was not able to save you all. God knows I tried. I pledge to you that Dogs Deserve Better will continue to fight for your rights, and there's a good chance that I'm not done fighting for you either.

You are not forgotten, and the world is changing. Soon dogs living as you have will be nothing but a distant memory, and those of us who fought for you will finally get to rest and say "Job well done." Today is not that day, but we will not give up. I love you. *

---

* Watch the video announcement at https://youtu.be/3ToOA6p-V3k

Misty after ditching her heavy logging chain, running in our field.

CHAPTER SIXTY-SEVEN:

A Tearful Goodbye

"DOGS DESERVE BETTER PUT DOGS FIRST. IT WAS REWARD-
ING TO BE ABLE TO REHABILITATE DOGS THAT HAVE BEEN
ABUSED AND SEE THEM GET ADOPTED BY LOVING FAMILIES,
GET A SECOND CHANCE AT LIFE. DDB WAS AN EXPERIENCE
OF A LIFETIME FOR ME, ONE I WILL NEVER FORGET. EVERY
DOG THAT CAME THROUGH THE FACILITY LEFT WITH A
PIECE OF MY HEART."—HEATHER PECKO, DOG CARETAKER

DDB staff member Amy Havens had planned a fundraiser
for the organization the weekend after my departure,
and so the event became my final, and very tearful, goodbye

to the organization and staff I loved. Amy and Donna Hughes co-wrote an incredibly moving song for the chained dogs, entitled *Why Me?*, which was sung and recorded by Bria Kelly of The Voice.*

Staff build their dog collar monument to my efforts for chained dogs.

Amy kept both the song and the staff's tribute to me a secret, so I had no idea what to expect, which made it all the more powerful. While Bria and her band played *Why Me?*, Amy and the rest of the DDB staff members walked across the front of the room, somberly layering collars from dogs we'd rescued onto a tabletop. The impromptu monument they created high-lighted our purpose, our mission on behalf of all the dogs who deserved better. **

It was exactly the tribute I'd have wished for, and my tears and the hugs I gave each staff member said more than my inad-equate vocabulary is capable of expressing. I felt an immense sense of gratitude for it all—the good and the bad—for the sor-rows shone a spotlight on that one moment of purity; I may not have appreciated the beautiful without the ugly.

In that moment, I truly believed that I'd given my best.

I'd come full circle.

I was done.

---

* Watch the official song video at https://youtu.be/byoPuFK5wNE
** Watch the tearful goodbye video at https://youtu.be/pFfwE6iTxdk

Matilda was now free. Maybe, so was I.

CHAPTER SIXTY-EIGHT:
The Aftermath

When I left the organization, I simply handed the reins to our new board president and walked away. I was worried I'd try to micromanage if I stayed on in any capacity, and so I just let it all go. The board had assured me they would continue the goals of the organization, up to and including our addition and new facility.

It was all I could ask for.

Unfortunately, it was not to be.

The new CEO quickly pulled a coup and ousted not only the board President, but the two dedicated DDB employees who made me feel safe enough to leave, Julie Sayre and Melody Whitworth.

Melody Whitworth sued the organization based on the contract we'd signed which allowed her to start her own official branch; the case was settled out of court for an undisclosed amount.

She founded and now runs her own organization in Columbia, Missouri, at unchainedmelodies.org.

Julie lost the organization and career she loved.

Today Julie tells me, "It's not often that a job can change your entire life. I never considered myself an activist for animals as I was looking for employment. That all changed when I read about the job opening as an office manager for Dogs Deserve Better. As I researched the organization before applying for the position, the opportunity quickly felt more like a calling than it did a job. I've never had a more meaningful, life-changing opportunity. The work I accomplished at DDB is truly something I will cherish for the rest of my life. I thank Tamira for the opportunity she gave me, and for everything she taught me."

The addition plans we'd approved for Stage Two of the project.

Due to the myriad obstacles I'd had to overcome, I'd only gotten us through Stage One of our 3-Stage Plan for the Good Newz Rehab Center: **Pay off the Property and House.**

In Stage Two we were slated to build a wing onto the existing home, which Mark Hyre had been working on with an architect. The drawings were amazing, though, as you can see, and it saddens me that this wing has never been built.

In Stage Three we were to build the dream facility: a state-of-the-art facility further back on the property, which would consist of small apartments to house and train as many as 50 dogs at a time to become loving family members.

Unfortunately, neither of these plans has been started or come to fruition, to my knowledge; nor have there been replacement plans outlined anywhere that I can see.

I left the organization in much better financial shape than I found it, since I started at zero. During my tenure with the organization, I raised over $4,000,000 for the chained dogs, paid off a 4,600 square foot facility and 16 acres (leaving my successors debt-free), and left approx. $150,000 in hand ($125,000 in cash holdings, and $25,000 in a fund account).

Given that the monthly budget at the time was approximately $20,000, this would have given new leadership six months free and clear to get back on their feet and running smoothly.

Dogs Deserve Better is still in operation and is still located at 1915 Moonlight Road. From what I can see, they are continuing to rescue and adopt out dogs from the home, but aren't doing much to raise their voices for the chained dogs on a national level.

The website is beautiful, though.

There was a point early on that the new organizational leadership intended to destroy the dog-fighting sheds. I stood against it then, and I would continue to do so now.

I've hosted tours of hundreds of visitors through those sheds; I've cried and I've watched others cry, as they were so touched by the plight of the fighting dog and so moved by what occurred there that their emotions overtook them.

Not a single person who went in there came out unaffected.

That is the power of those sheds.

The sheds as I found them my first day on the property, February 1, 2011.

When boy scout Tyler Ducar chose Dogs Deserve Better and the preservation of these sheds as his eagle project, it was because he recognized the value of this memorial landmark to all dog-loving Americans.

His reward for this hard work and for the teens and adults who helped him would be the destruction of that which he sought to help preserve. DDB gave our word to Tyler that we would continue to make these sheds into the landmark and museum they deserve to be.

The organization needs to stand by its word.

Not only that, but who would benefit most from the sheds being destroyed? Michael Vick, because the last remaining evidence of his abuse would be gone.

It was explained to me that DDB leadership wanted the sheds destroyed because they're ugly. **Yes, they are ugly. They are a stark and brutal reminder of what happens in the dogfighting world.**

And that's exactly the point.

Please join me in advocating for those sheds to officially become a memorial museum of the cruelty that occurred on the property; they serve and can continue to serve as a much-needed educational tool for how society can do better.

Two positive developments on the property include the installation of an above-ground swimming pool for the dogs, and the planting of a tree in the field for each of the Vick dogs who were rescued—an amazing idea that touched the dogs' adopters and all those who loved and followed them.

I hope that someone will come along with tons of energy, dreams, and connections, and will move the organization in a dramatically positive direction, tackling the addition and the dream facility . . .

I'd hate to think the price I paid for their freedom from abuse was all for naught.

At the end of 2014, Gerald Poindexter made the news himself.

From local station WTKR:

James City County, Va.—Police arrested Surry County Commonwealth's Attorney Gerald Glen Poindexter Saturday, charging him with driving under the influence.

James City County Police say they were initially called around 3:40 p.m. for a car accident involving an intoxicated driver.

The accident took place at the Jamestown Ferry Dock on the Surry side of the James River Ferry. Investigators report that Poindexter's car struck a curb while loading onto the ferry. Employees of the ferry tried to stop Poindexter's car, but say he kept going and hit a car.

James City County Police met with Poindexter once the ferry arrived at the Jamestown dock. Police say Poindexter was arrested for driving under the influence and no driver's license in possession.

According to a warrant obtained by NewsChannel 3, Poindexter was given six field sobriety tests, and "failed them completely." [*]

---

[*] https://wtkr.com/2014/11/29/surry-county-commonwealth-attorney-arrested-for-

In addition, the officer wrote in his arrest warrant, "Mr. Poindexter was given an opportunity to use the restroom, but urinated on himself while in the restroom."

Well, that's just awkward.

I often wondered what I would say or do if Michael Vick tried to donate or visit. His money was tainted, yet at the same time it was clear that he owed the dogs . . . a lot. Whether or not to accept money from the man was a moral dilemma that I had no ready answer for, but it was also one that I never had to face.

He never tried to donate a dime.

They were just "f@*cking dogs", after all.

Mark Hyre and I eventually became friendly again. He wrote me (and the organization) the following amends, which I've promised to add to the book:

"Tami, I want to again thank you for taking a chance on me and I apologize for letting you, the staff, and the dogs down. It was not my 'demons' that caused it; alcoholism is a symptom, not the cause. I own full responsibility for my failure there; I lost your friendship, Laurel, my self-respect, and the respect of the staff at DDB. I am looking at a future of being sick, broke, alone, and apparently unemployable.

"My cancer went into remission two years ago, then came back with a vengeance last summer. Now I am stage 3 cancer in my throat and liver, plus I have cirrhosis, copd, long term bi-polar disorder, and had a heart valve replaced with a pig valve (I don't eat bacon anymore).

"I don't blame anyone or anything—I had every opportunity

driving-under-the-influence/

in my life, and all this is self-inflicted. You were/are a very important part of my life.

" I wish I was still part of DDB, but I appreciate that I was at all; I just made it too short a time."

I will always be proud of the accomplishments I made for the chained dogs through my time with DDB. I did my best:

• From September 2005 (our first 990 IRS filing) through June 2015, DDB raised $3,945,761 for the cause and paid out $623,767 in vet care costs for rescued chained and penned dogs all across America and into other countries. In addition, our Hero Fund Vet Care Grant provided initial veterinary care for 229 dogs from October 2012 through October 2015 at a total cost of $68,700. That's a lot of HAPPY—and FREE—DOGS!

• From August 2011 until April 2015, DDB rescued and rehabilitated more than 200 dogs from the house at the Good Newz Rehab Center. I fostered at least 250 dogs from my home before moving to the center, and nationwide other volunteers and reps rescued thousands of dogs from chains and pens, even starting or inspiring other local groups in many areas.

• I spent 878 hours chained to a doghouse on behalf of those without a voice, and spoke in front of state committees and local communities on behalf of laws limiting chaining.

• The organization mailed or hand delivered at least 121,575 Valentines made by schoolchildren, groups, and volunteers to chained dogs nationwide from 2006-2015. We mailed educational brochures all year long, every year, to dog caretakers offering our services on behalf of their dogs.

Matilda: this is what peace looks like.

CHAPTER SIXTY-NINE:

Recommendations for those Suffering Defamation in the Animal Rescue Movement

*M*ost folks don't leave rescue because of the animals, although compassion fatigue is very real, and it affects many who work in the field. The more animals you care for, the harder your life becomes. That's just a fact. Yet, I would wager the single greatest cause of good people leaving the movement is the defamation by those who, for whatever reason, seek to destroy others, both online and through the use and manipulation of local authorities.

This is typically accomplished via accusations of monetary theft from the nonprofit, or accusations of cruelty to animals.

Sometimes both.

If you're undergoing defamation on top of the day-to-day strain of caring for the animals, it can quickly throw you into depression, and a feeling of helplessness and hopelessness can take hold. At this point, you're headed for a crisis situation.

If money is not an issue for you, and you can afford to sue the pants off of them, consider doing it. Bullies are cowards . . . when the going gets tough, they pack up and go find an easier mark. Not only that, but in our online world, bullies often gather a group of minions to do their dirty work for them. Once those minions scatter, the bully's power is greatly diminished.

Most sycophants WILL run for the hills once court action starts.

Suing, of course, involves a lot of evidence collection; and, if you lose the case in court, it will send more trauma your way. If the bully wins, they are empowered and the abuse will escalate.

Wading in and collecting evidence of the defamation also exacerbates your trauma. Ensure you are in therapy or have a great self-plan in place before doing so. It's ugly and painful to read the lies these folks put out there about you.

One of the Sandy Hook fathers sued and won $450,000, but he's spent years and an untold amount in the course of fighting back. Lenny Pozner was quoted in the Washington Post as saying, "The damages awarded me for Mr. Fetzer's prolific defamation and harassment are significant, not so much for the dollar amount, which I will likely never see due to Mr. Fetzer's economic reality, but for the precedent that it sets. This sends a message to hoaxers and conspiracy theorists and others, who seek to use the Internet to revictimize and terrorize vulnerable people, that their actions have consequences. When you defame people online, that has consequences." [8]

Given today's internet situation and the empowerment of those with personality disorders and malicious tendencies to go after those they perceive as having "wronged" them, you have to find a way to work around these people. Defamers will never totally disappear; worst of all, they almost always have severe mental afflictions that allow them to lie and manipulate public sentiment against you without a shred of guilt or remorse.

How does one even combat that kind of conscienceless behavior?

The damage they seek to inflict can be neutralized in the public view by making the facts readily available. Highlight your annual 990 IRS forms on your website, show photos of all your dogs.

Most importantly, invite people IN! If you have nothing to hide, hide nothing.

Depending on the situation, I would also suggest hiring someone, a third party, to investigate. Maybe a retired police officer or a private investigator who loves animals. This person would show up—at an undisclosed time—at your property to inspect everything, take photos, and interview staff and volunteers. Then they would attempt to speak with the people who are defaming you, asking them for evidence of their claims—they don't usually have any, thriving on insinuations and promises of evidence "to come".

It would behoove you to make the resulting evaluation public, or at a minimum provide it to those who email you about the situation. Hopefully this evaluation would exonerate you, or at worst point out a few areas you could improve in, thereby discrediting those who are trying to destroy you.

Another thing to check for? Criminal records. Many of those who have no compunction about destroying others have criminal records or other such reports of bad behavior. Do a background check.

Bullies love an easy target. Unfortunately those of us who work with and for the animals are sensitive souls; these kinds of wounds slice deeply and do lasting harm to your emotional well-being.

Remember to showcase all your happy animals and testimonials! It will at least give you a fighting chance.

I wish you all the best of luck.

Dogs like Hef got to know freedom and love because of Dogs Deserve Better.

CHAPTER SEVENTY:
What You Can Learn from My Mistakes

"AT TIMES OUR LIGHT GOES OUT, AND IS REKINDLED BY A SPARK FROM ANOTHER PERSON. EACH OF US HAS CAUSE TO THINK WITH DEEP GRATITUDE OF THOSE WHO HAVE LIGHTED THE FLAME WITHIN US."—ALBERT SCHWEITZER

As humans, we don't see the mistakes we're making until they're in the rearview mirror, or we wouldn't make them in the first place. If you're in the rescue world, might I suggest you read my tale as a cautionary one, and make wiser choices that I did.

Although I still believe that buying Vick's property was an amazing activist move—we took a place where dogs were casually destroyed and gave the property back to the abused—the corruption that led Vick to know he could get away with dog-fighting there should have stopped me from thinking it was a good idea.

Why go somewhere that you aren't wanted, or worse, where they will use every trick in the book to rid themselves of you and your organization?

It's hard enough to get a facility off the ground, to build a place for your animals that is healthy for them, both physically and mentally, and healthy for you, too. But if people with an axe to grind can conspire with county officials who want you gone? Your life will indeed churn downward into one long, hell-ish nightmare.

Don't do it to yourself.

Find a place where you're welcome, where the beautiful work you're doing for the animals is appreciated, and where you can work together as a community to build something suc-cessful.

In terms of staffing, do your background checks, and believe those red flags when you see them. Many of us are so desper-ate for help, we allow people with sociopathic agendas into our organizations. They will do all in their power to destroy you as soon as you make them angry—and given that they live in a state of perpetual anger, it won't take long.

I recommend Dr. Phil's book *Life Code: New Rules for the Real World,* for those who want to learn what to look for in scammers and schemers. We have to be smarter if we don't want to take a fall at the hands of those with nefarious intent.

And lastly, take care of yourself. No one person can save the world. Have you done your share? When is it enough?

Only you will know the answers to these questions.

For rescue or sanctuary owners going through the pain of defamation and online bullying, I suggest the following self-help regimen:

1. If you are in an emotional crisis, please seek profes-

sional help. Sometimes the trauma of the abuse can simply be overwhelming. Having someone to talk to each week—who isn't involved in the drama and is paid to listen to you—is therapeutic. When you don't know who you can trust, the confidentiality provided by these sessions gives you a safe place to release the pain (and tears) you've been holding in at work.

The dogs were grateful and FREE.

2. Tapping. For between sessions, or for those who cannot afford to go to therapy, I recommend tapping. It can be done with just you, in a few minutes per day, AND there is a free tutorial website by the founder of the method, Gary Craig, you can use to train yourself.

Tapping is a way to release negative emotions. Even when we THINK we are holding up well in the face of defamation and abuse, the negative emotions, shame, and guilt piled onto our shoulders can be devastating.

Start your tapping journey here, and let go of the pain each day. https://www.emofree.com (Here you can download his free e-book.)

(P.S. I receive no compensation of any kind for this plug . . . I just use tapping on a daily basis, and I know it's helpful for me.)

The official tutorial lessons start here: https://www.emo-free.com/english/eft-tapping-tutorial-en.html

3. After you've done your tapping for the day, bring some positivity back into your life by keeping a gratitude journal. This is a simple daily exercise that helps you focus on the good in life, once you've let go of some of the hurtful. This exercise will only take minutes a day. To do: make a list of ten items you're grateful for, in the following format. "I am grateful for _____, because _____."

Use your journal to express gratitude for things you've already received (i.e. I am grateful for my beautiful home, because I have a safe place to sleep at night) or things you would LIKE to receive, pretending that you have them already (i.e. I am grateful for a $1,000,000 donation for my organization, because then we are FREE!).

What's most important about the gratitude list is that you FEEL GOOD when you write it. So dream big, and bring up some true feelings of happiness to pour onto the page.

Jada, looking for critters in the field. She and Copper got their very own home—together.

Epilogue

"I EVENTUALLY CAME TO THIS POINT WHERE I REALIZED THAT I COULDN'T RUN AWAY FROM WHAT HAPPENED TO ME. I HAD TO INTEGRATE IT. WHAT IT ALSO MEANS IS THAT ANYBODY CAN DO THIS. THIS CAN HAPPEN FOR ANYBODY, YOU DON'T HAVE TO GO THROUGH A GLOBAL SCANDAL. I THINK THAT NO MATTER WHAT YOUR HUMILIATIONS ARE OR SETBACKS, YOU CAN FIND A WAY TO HAVE A DIFFERENT ENDING TO YOUR STORY."—MONICA LEWINSKY [9]

I'm relieved to get this book out of my head and onto the page, to finally finish a beautiful yet conversely irredeemably ugly chapter of my life. For years this story has weighed me down, the pain of going back into the events of that time too much to relive. I couldn't do it.

I don't know if anyone will read my story, but for me the freedom comes in the release; I find it no longer matters whether it's read by the few or by the many.

It is done.

The ending has dissipated the pain, at least in part.

After leaving the organization, I spent a year in therapy, diagnosed with PTSD and compassion fatigue syndrome. I never would have imagined the gut-wrenching anguish caused by the false charges, and the resulting shame that would rocket through every facet of my being.

I realized I would probably never work in an animal organization again, even if I wanted to, because I'd been accused of cruelty to those we serve. Although the charges were false and we'd beat them in court, the stigma would remain.

The grief of this loss was overwhelming.

I felt adrift.

In the end we'd won, but I certainly didn't feel like I had.

Won the right to what? To exist? Everyone should have that basic right without having to fight for it.

Even today I observe in myself a need to prove to others that my companion animals are still alive, still thriving. I'm afraid that underneath it all, people are wondering if I'm beating them behind closed doors, or killing and replacing them with look-alikes on a regular basis.

You know, just to fool everyone and get away with my evil plots.

Logically I know these fears are irrational, that most folks either don't remember, never knew, or never believed the lies in the first place; yet the ongoing terror is part of the PTSD symptoms I carry, and these fears often raise their heads when I least expect them.

The terror is almost great enough for me to live without companion animals, but I would miss them so very much. Dogs and cats have been part of my life for too many years to give them up, so I choose instead to cope with the ambivalence.

I also avoided writing the book for so long because I knew

I would have to be open and honest—vulnerable—about many of the harder things I went through, about all of it. This would give Deana, Fiala, and Poindexter great joy, because they would see that they were more successful in their missions to destroy me than they realized. They didn't—and don't—deserve that satisfaction.

I'm glad I managed to save DDB from their clutches, even if I was broken in the process.

Today I engage in more solitary pursuits, writing and occasionally doing events for our books.

Trump's presidency was massively triggering for me, as he reminds me of each of my tormentors, all wrapped together and on steroids. I knew that if he won the election I would spend the following years witnessing what he was doing to others and our country, but feeling hopeless to stop it.

I understand why so many of those who've been abused ended up back in therapy when the man was elected.

I didn't know how I could help the animals after leaving the organization, but I went back to my roots and figured out a new way to be useful. Before founding and building Dogs Deserve Better, I was an art director, mainly crafting book covers and interiors for a living. I had written, edited, and designed four books while running the nonprofit, so I decided I could (and would) start a publishing company for animal lovers.

I call the company Who Chains You Books, a nod to both the animals and the ordeal I will always carry with me; I began official operations in the summer of 2016.

Doing so has allowed me to help the cause without being on the front lines, given me a way to make a difference without being falsely accused of harming animals or stealing my organization's money. I had to protect myself from that abuse.

As of this writing, I've published more than 75 books in the first four years, many of them children's books, about all kinds of animals. It's wonderful to see the excitement of the authors when their book is ready for the world, and I hope our tales make a difference in the lives of our readers and ultimately the voiceless they serve.

My life is now quieter, and calmer, and kinder.

I live on a river, and the message of the river is always that this too shall pass; the bad comes and goes, and the river adapts and changes right along with it.

I feed the birds, squirrels, and other small critters, cuddle with my cats, and walk my dog Khronos along our lane in all kinds of weather.

There is peace now.

I would say namaste, but that sounds a bit too cliché, and like I'm cooler than I am.

So I'll just say I wish you all the best.

Except those who gleefully harm others.

You, maybe not so much.

Jada and Copper in their home together, "helping" dad play videogames.

Acknowledgments

There are so many people who played a part, positive and negative, in those four years. I worry I will miss some who deserve a shout out.

First and foremost, my thanks and appreciation go to Dr. Leslie Dragon. Even though, as a mobile vet, she'd been to our center numerous times before that fateful day, she could have told me "Sorry, I don't want to get involved." But she didn't; she took the much harder step of doing what was right. Dr. Dragon exclaimed on her second visit that the place was amazing, and that she was really happy for the dogs who got a chance for a new life with us. She testified when it mattered most, saving both Jada and me from an uncertain fate. I can never thank her enough.

To Samantha Laine, who forced me to stand and fight, and Mark Kumpf, who lent me his expert opinion, support, and advice. I am grateful.

To Joe, who I suspect suffered his own PTSD from watching me go through it all. When I melted down, he melted down right beside me. And then we'd eat Taco Bell. When you love someone, it's hard to watch them hurt and feel helpless to fix it. Thanks for being my shoulder to cry on.

To my two heart volunteers, the ladies who faithfully showed up through the hardest parts, Leslie Thibeault and Melanie Gilbert. They gave of their weekends to the dogs, and their kindness and empathy to me. You will always hold a place in my heart.

A big thanks to all the other volunteers who came even once to lend a hand. Each and every one of you helped us move forward on a very large undertaking. I am grateful. Special thanks to the following for their early and ongoing support: Larry Oxton, Michele Oxton, Angela Brown, Reg Green, and Jo Vance.

To the staff members who DIDN'T frame me OR steal our money: You did the hard work, and you loved the dogs, which was all I could ask of you, and the best each of us could do. Together we believed in a cause and we worked together to make something beautiful from the ugly. Thank you to Julie, Jay, Heather, Amy, Zeko, Melissa, Corrie, Nick, Tim, Mark, Nicki, Sherri, Megan, Kirsten, Kristina, Cara, Chris, Tracey, and Chrissy.

To Monica, thank you for fundraising with us, donating to get us on our feet, and giving me valuable business insight. You inspired me to move forward, and I am grateful.

This book may have not had the "happy" ending it did without the generosity of benefactors Ransom T. McCarty and Peggy & Eric Lieber. I hope if you're looking down from above, you can see the depths of gratitude in my heart for including us in your bequests. You gave our dogs a home.

To Deb Carr and Melody Whitworth, thanks for your years of professionalism and caring; you did Dogs Deserve Better proud.

To all the folks who represented us over the years as volunteer Area Reps, thank you for saving those you could. Even though we never got them all, it wasn't for lack of trying.

To the authors I'm honored to work with today, and the

humane workers and nonprofits who take our books to the kids, thanks for helping the animals through education.

I'd be remiss if I didn't give a shout out to the Culpeper PoGo group, who taught me there is play after heartbreak, friendship through cooperation, and places where folks of all ages and walks of life can laugh (and shiny hunt) together.

And last but never least, I thank my kids Rayne and Bryn and my beloved companion animals who stuck with me through all the years of DDB. My love for you tethers me to this earth. I love you.

One of my favorite center dogs, Spotty, often traveled with me because he loved to climb the fence and take himself on walkabouts. I love this picture of him and I. He helped me believe.

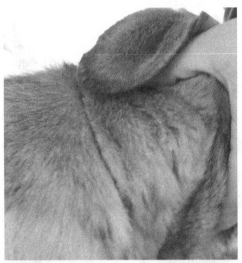

Abby came to us with still-fresh scarring and wounds from an embedded collar. Soon she was flirting and loving her new life and caring family.

Before & After Rescue Photos

Angel left her chained-life behind, even visiting my home in northern Virginia where she swam in the river and relaxed in the sun on our back deck with Sloan.

Before & After Rescue Photos

Betty White was just a sweet little old lady; pics show
the difference just a few weeks of basic care can make.

Before & After Rescue Photos

Bernard lived in the mud in a rickety old doghouse. He was grateful every day for the intervention of his rescuers and DDB.

Before & After Rescue Photos

The conditions that humans force our best friends into can be shocking. Copper was skeletal, with a dirty "pool" for water and way too little food before his rescue.

Before & After Rescue Photos

Diamond was adopted by a local family who doted on her; even though her before photo is so very sad, her after photo as she chased a ball through the field—healthy and happy—says it all.

Before & After Rescue Photos

We ended up with
five hound puppies
from Surry County,
Virginia, who
were starving
and nothing but
skin and bones.

Not for long!

Before & After Rescue Photos

Pepper had her puppies on a West Virginia chain. By the time they came to us, there were only two puppies left. She quickly learned that the morning walks were an excellent way to start the day with her new friends!

Before & After Rescue Photos

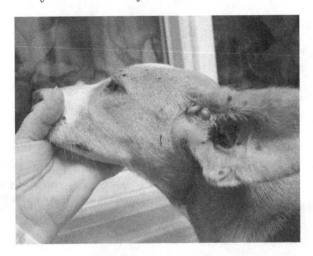

Three more hound pups arrived covered in ticks.
Dog caretaker Chris got a kiss of gratitude for all his help.

Before & After Rescue Photos

Shaggy was an old guy with matted fur and aching joints, but nothing stopped him from reveling in his first taste of freedom.

Field Runs & Play Dates

I got so much joy out of watching dogs we'd freed from inhumane conditions race through the fields and play with new friends; after all, isn't that what every dog deserves?

EXPANDED EDITION

Field Runs & Play Dates

ENDNOTES

1. Kathy Strouse, *Badd News: The Untold Story of the Michael Vick Dog Fighting Case*, (2009), 127.

2. Jim Gorant, *The Lost Dogs: Michael Vick's Dogs and Their Tale of Rescue and Redemption*, (New York: Gotham Books, 2010), 30.

3. "Dark tourism, explained: Why visitors flock to sites of tragedy." The Washington Post, November 13, 2019, https://www.washingtonpost.com/graphics/2019/travel/dark-tourism-explainer/

4. https://www.cnn.com/2019/10/17/politics/william-mcraven-trump-cnntv/index.html

5. Cheryl Dellasega, Ph.D, *Mean Girls Grown Up: Adult Women Who Are Still Queen Bees, Middle Bees, and Afraid-to-Bees*, (Wiley, 2005)

6. Martha Stout, Ph.D, *The Sociopath Next Door: The Ruthless Versus the Rest of Us*, (New York: Broadway Books, 2005), 4.

7. Kathy Strouse, *Badd News: The Untold Story of the Michael Vick Dog Fighting Case*, (2009), 56.

8. https://www.washingtonpost.com/education/2019/10/16/jury-awards-father-sandy-hook-victim-defamation-case/

9. https://www.aol.com/article/news/2019/10/16/monica-lewinsky-impeachment-inquiry-were-all-affected/23838745/

BIBLIOGRAPHY

Dellasega, Cheryl, Ph.D. (2005). *Mean Girls Grown Up: Adult Women Who Are Still Queen Bees, Middle Bees, and Afraid-to-Bees*. New York: Wiley.

Gorant, Jim. (2010). *The Lost Dogs: Michael Vick's Dogs and Their Tale of Rescue and Redemption*. New York: Gotham Books.

McGraw, Phillip C. (2012). *Life Code: New Rules for the Real World*. Los Angeles: Bird Street Books.

Stout, Martha, Ph.D. (2005). *The Sociopath Next Door: The Ruthless Versus the Rest of Us*. New York: Broadway Books.

Strouse, Kathy. (2009). *Badd News: The Untold Story of the Michael Vick Dog Fighting Case*. Fighting Investigation Publications LLC.

Additional online sources:

Washington Post
Wikipedia
Roanoke Times
CNN
Yahoo Sports
Aol News
WTKR

Thank you for taking the time
to read *It Went to the Dogs*

Could you take a moment to give the book
a short review on Amazon.com? Your reviews
mean the world to our authors, and help
stories such as this one reach a wider
audience. Thank you so much!

Find links to
It Went to the Dogs
and all our great books
on Amazon or at www.whochainsyou.com.

ABOUT THE *Author*

Tamira Thayne pioneered the anti-tethering movement in America, forming and leading the nonprofit Dogs Deserve Better for 13 years.

During her time on the front lines of animal activism and rescue she took on plenty of bad guys (often failing miserably); her swan song culminated in the purchase and transformation of Michael Vick's dogfighting compound to a chained-dog rescue and rehabilitation center. She's spent 878 hours chained to a doghouse on behalf of the voiceless in front of state capitol buildings nationwide.

Tamira is the author of the Chained Gods series, the Animal Protectors Series, *Foster Doggie Insanity*, and *Capitol in Chains*. She's the editor of *More Rescue Smiles*, and the co-editor of *Unchain My Heart* and *Rescue Smiles*. In 2016 she founded Who Chains You, publishing books by and for animal activists and rescuers.

Tamira is an Air Force veteran who lives by a river in the woods of northern Virginia, with her husband, daughter, one dog, six cats, and hundreds of outside birds and critters she adores from afar.

Foster Doggie Insanity: Tips & Tales to Keep Your Kool as a Doggie Foster Parent

Do you struggle as a doggie foster parent, and feel like you're the only one who finds it hard? Do you want to foster a dog, but don't know where to start, how to prepare, and what to expect? If so, this is the book for you. Described by one reader as "an embrace from a friend who understands what we all go through. It is a beacon of hope to let other rescuers know that they are not alone. It is a must read for anyone involved in rescue."

The image you see on the cover of this book is not 'real' life. It's how Thayne wishes doggie foster parenting could be—but fostering is not for wimps, cowards, or the otherwise mess-or-insanity-challenged. It's hard and emotionally draining work, and there are days we all could use an understanding shoulder to cry on.

You are not alone! *Let Foster Doggie Insanity* be there for you.

...Read more and order from whochainsyou.com, Amazon, and other outlets.

Also from Tamira Thayne

CAPITOL IN CHAINS:
54 DAYS OF THE DOGHOUSE BLUES

In August 2010, one woman carried a doghouse to the steps of the Pennsylvania State Capitol building and chained herself to it, seeking passage of a law protecting dogs from life at the end of a chain.

Not knowing if she'd be arrested, ignored, or ridiculed, she set aside her fears and acted on behalf of the voiceless: dogs—the most social of beings—whose needs have been overlooked by those with the power to create chain-ge for their future.

This is her story, and the story of the 54 days she and others spent chained at the bottom of the Capitol steps in Harrisburg, Pennsylvania. May you be inspired, entertained, and educated about the needs of Man's Best Friend, and how these needs continue to be negated in today's society.

Second Edition Includes:

Updates on PA Laws

The Doghouse Wedding

Eleven Years of Chain Off in America

...*Read more and order from whochainsyou.com, Amazon, and other outlets.*

Also from Tamira Thayne

THE ANIMAL PROTECTOR SERIES

In this refreshing new series, the animals take steps to become their own heroes, and find their freedom again with the aid of caring people. Perfect for ages 8 and up.

THE RESCUE SMILES SERIES

The heart of the animal rescue world lies in its stories—of freedom, of love, and of sacrifice by those who not only acknowledge but embrace the human-animal bond and its wondrous gifts.

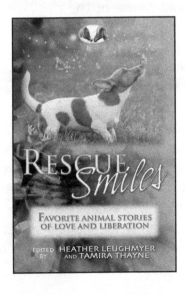

I Once Was Lost, But Now I'm Found: Daisy and the Olympic Animal Sanctuary Rescue

On the far side of the Olympic Peninsula in Washington State, halfway between the mountains and the ocean, stands the little town of Forks. In that town, in a quiet neighborhood of modest homes and shabby businesses, there remains a dilapidated pink warehouse.

Packed inside that warehouse, living in deplorable conditions, were once over 120 dogs. Some of the dogs were kept in crates piled high on shelves, arranged in rows along the walls, and shoved into corners behind heaps of garbage and urine-saturated straw. Some of the dogs were confined to wire-sided or glassed-in kennels. One was kept in an old horse trailer. Dead ones were stored in a cooler.

In one of the crates was a black dog named Daisy. This is her story. It is also the story of the rescue of one hundred and twenty-four dogs—and one snake—from the Olympic Animal Sanctuary, the only large-scale dog rescue in the U.S. to be carried out with no support from local government. The OAS rescue was an epic narrative that extended over several years and featured small town politics, protests, assault, lawsuits, arrests, and a midnight escape, all played out to a nationwide audience....*Read more and order from whochainsyou.com, Amazon, and other outlets.*

About Who Chains You Books

WELCOME TO WHO CHAINS YOU: BOOKS FOR THOSE WHO BELIEVE PEOPLE—AND ANIMALS— DESERVE TO BE FREE.

At Who Chains You Books our mission is a simple one—to amplify the voices of the animals through the empowerment of animal lovers, activists, and rescuers to write and publish books elevating the status of animals in today's society.

We hope you'll visit our website and join us on this adventure we call animal advocacy publishing. We welcome you.

Read more about us at whochainsyou.com.